LET'S TALK SLANG

*A Glossary of **Gen Z & Alpha Words***

DR. RINCY SAJI

Dedication

To anyone who hasn't realized 'bet' is more than a wager and 'no cap' means way more than a missing hat.

Contents

About the Author

Dr. Rincy Saji is an Assistant Professor in the Department of Languages at Rajagiri College of Social Sciences (Autonomous), Kalamassery, Kerala. She earned her Ph.D. in English Language and Literature from Mahatma Gandhi University, Kottayam, and has been recognized for her academic excellence, including securing the NTA NET/JRF in 2020. Her scholarly interests encompass a diverse range of fields, including cultural studies, post-humanism, post-colonialism, digital literature, and war studies. She has made significant contributions to her field through numerous publications in both national and international journals, including those indexed by UGC-CARE, Scopus, and Web of Science.

Acknowledgments

Let's Talk Slang: A Glossary of Gen Z/Alpha Words is a testament to the dynamic and collaborative nature of teaching and learning. This book would not have been possible without the invaluable contributions of my students, whose insights and enthusiasm helped me navigate the ever-evolving world of contemporary slang. From clarifying that *'cap'* is now synonymous with *'lie'* to revealing that *'ate'* signifies doing something flawlessly, their inputs opened my eyes to a fascinating new mode of communication.

I extend my deepest gratitude to my students, particularly Mr. Dil Jacob Thomas (BBA HRM, 2024–2028) and Mr. Saifan Subin (IMCA, 2024–2029) of Rajagiri College of Social Sciences (Autonomous), Kerala. Dil's extensive research contributions and thoughtful engagement were instrumental in shaping the glossary, truly making him a co-collaborator in this endeavor. Saifan's creative illustrations brought the spirit of this book to life, adding a unique and engaging visual layer that I couldn't have envisioned alone.

I am also profoundly thankful to Dr. Achamma Alex, Head of the Department of Languages at Rajagiri College of Social Sciences (Autonomous), for her constant encouragement and valuable guidance throughout this journey. Her support and faith in my work motivated me at every stage of this project.

Special thanks to my colleague Mr. Noel Simon Roy, Assistant Professor in the Department of Commerce, Rajagiri College of Social Sciences whose unwavering encouragement and insights during the initial stages of this book were pivotal in turning an idea into a reality.

I owe a heartfelt thanks to Isha and the team at Notion Publishers for their professionalism and dedication. Their guidance and belief in this project ensured its successful publication, bringing my vision to life in ways I could not have imagined.

This book was inspired by a desire to bridge generational gaps and foster understanding between educators, parents, and anyone curious about the language of today's youth. As a teacher, I have often spent extended hours explaining complex concepts. However, exploring Gen Z and Alpha slang revealed an incredible cultural shift—these generations prioritize brevity, creativity, and speed in their communication. Terms like *'sus'* (suspicious) and acronyms like *'IDK'* (I Don't Know) highlight their ingenuity and desire for efficiency. This revelation sparked my curiosity and inspired a deep dive into their linguistic world.

Finally, I am deeply grateful to you, the readers, for embarking on this journey with me. I hope this book not only enriches your understanding of contemporary slang but also brings a smile to your face. After all, language is as fluid and fun as a viral TikTok trend, with meanings shifting and evolving as quickly as the world around us.

Note

I remember a defining moment in my journey as a parent when my daughter, Ezlyn Iva's first words weren't "Amma" or "Appa" (Mom and Dad in Malayalam), but rather "ale-k-chha…" (/əˈlɛk.tʃə/) for Amazon Alexa. It was not unexpected, though, given the environment she grew up in. In our home, instead of lullabies, it was Alexa who used to sing the songs for her. This was a clear testament to how deeply technology has seeped into our everyday lives and how naturally the next generation connects with the virtual world around them. But it's not just the involvement of technology; their vocabulary has also evolved. Words and expressions that didn't exist a few years ago are now common, and what may seem foreign to us is second nature to them. Their language has adapted to the fast-paced, digital world they inhabit, often filled with acronyms, abbreviations, and entirely new slang that reflects the world they live in.

This shift in communication patterns is particularly challenging in my English classrooms. As a teacher, I've had to adapt to the new world my students inhabit—a world where traditional forms of language and grammar often seem secondary. My students often converse in a language that is constantly changing, influenced by social media trends, viral content, and the rapid exchange of ideas online. Acronyms like TMI (Too Much Information), FOMO (Fear of Missing Out), and phrases like *rizz, sigma*, or *no cap* have become second nature to them, making it an exciting yet challenging for someone like me, who is deeply invested in language's formal structures and traditional usage. They have taught me that language is not static—it evolves, grows, and adapts to the times.

Although, in the beginning, I restrained my students from using Gen Z/Alpha slang in classrooms and for personal conversations, I later came to understand that this shift is legitimate. Language, after all, is ever-evolving. Just as English has undergone significant transformations over centuries—from Old English, with words like 'hwæt' (meaning 'what') and 'cyning' (meaning 'king'), to Middle English, where 'gode' (meaning 'good') and 'hous' (meaning 'house'), to Modern English with words like 'beautiful' and 'freedom'—this is yet another period of linguistic shift. For instance, while 'thou' and 'thee' were once the standard forms of addressing someone informally in Old English, these gave way to the more familiar 'you' in Modern English. Similarly, in today's digital world, words like *lit* and *fam* are gaining traction in everyday conversation. This, in its essence, is the language's inevitable evolution.

The rise of Gen Z slang may just be another phase in this ongoing linguistic transformation. Understanding this change is crucial, as it reflects the fluidity of language and its adaptation to contemporary culture, just as language has shifted through the ages—from the epic poetry of Homer to the imagist poetry of Ezra Pound, and now, to the latest trends, like Instagram poetry (popularised by Rupi Kaur). As language evolves, it is essential to embrace these shifts, recognizing them as legitimate markers of cultural progression.

From Blighty to Bussin: Language Through the Ages

You know you've officially entered the 21ˢᵗ century where *lit* no longer refers to a light bulb, and *savage* no longer describes a wild animal. Language, once a static element of human communication, is now evolving faster than ever before, and if you're not paying attention, you might just miss some of the most significant—and often amusing—expressions emerging from the younger generations. If you've ever found yourself puzzled by terms like *slaps*, *bussin'*, *ohio*, or *sus*, you're not alone. This book is here to guide you through the dynamic and creative world of Gen Z and Gen Alpha slang and acronyms.

The Generational Divide: A Journey Through Language

Language is a living, evolving entity. Each generation adds its flavor to the vernacular, often shaped by the cultural, technological, and social contexts of the time. From the **Greatest Generation (born 1901-1927)**, who lived through the hardships of the World Wars and the Great Depression, came phrases like *blighty*, referring to home with a sense of longing during wartime, and *catch-22*, a paradoxical situation that became synonymous with bureaucratic absurdity, especially during military service. On the same note, phrases like *old hat* (meaning something is no longer fresh or exciting) and *clutch* (originally referring to an action taken in a critical moment, especially in sports) became part of their everyday speech. Words from this generation often carried a sense of simplicity and directness, matching the times they lived in.

The Silent Generation (born 1928-1945), influenced by the post-war climate and the need for stability, contributed to a more reserved and traditional way of speaking. Words like *in a jiffy* (quickly), denoting the civilian efforts that supported the war, and *gobbledygook* (nonsense), referring to the small gardens cultivated to help with wartime food shortages, encapsulated the spirit of community resilience. **The Baby Boomers (born 1946-1964),** emerging in the wake of World War II, brought about social change and cultural upheaval. Their language was filled with optimism, rebellion, and the beginnings of counterculture, with expressions like *groovy* and *Turkey* (a use-less or dim-witted person) reflective of the era's music, fashion, and growing social movements. As **Generation X (born 1965-1980)** came of age during the rise of technology and the internet, their language adopted a tone of cynicism and irony. The language during this time began to reflect a more cynical, sceptical attitude, with phrases like *radical* (meaning something extraordinary or impressive) and *chill* (used to describe a relaxed or laid-back attitude). By the time we reach the **Millennials (born 1981-1996),** technology has fully transformed the way people interact with the world. Influenced by the early days of the digital world and platforms like Facebook and Twitter, their vocabulary included terms like "LOL" (laughing out loud) and *selfie*, expressions that spoke to the growing influence of online interactions and the culture of self-expression. This generation brought the term *basic* into the common vernacular, used to describe someone or something that is perceived as unoriginal, predictable, or mainstream. These words symbolised a shift toward prioritizing experiences over materialism.

In today's world, it's **Gen Z (born 1996-2012) and *Gen Alpha* (born 2013-)** who are taking language to a whole new level, blending creativity, digital culture, and instant communication into a constantly evolving lexicon. Perhaps one of the most significant changes in language from Gen Z and Gen Alpha is their preference for words that are shorter, more impactful, and easier to communicate in the fast-moving digital world. The rise of social media platforms like TikTok has influenced these generations to favour quick, punchy phrases over long-winded explanations.

Gen Z or Generation Z, they are the first generation to grow up entirely immersed in the digital world. Their vocabulary reflects this digital-first existence, full of abbreviations, slang, and references that often require a bit of decoding. Take the word *savage*, for instance. While older generations might use it to describe something truly wild or untamed, Gen Z uses it to describe someone who does something so bold and unapologetic that it's almost impressive. A person might say, "Did you see how she stood up to her boss like that? She's *savage*!" Another popular Gen Z term is *bet*. While this word originally came from the world of gambling, Gen Z uses it to mean "okay" or "sure." If a friend says, "Let's go to the mall tomorrow," and you agree, you might respond with, *Bet.* It's simple, quick, and straight to the point. And who could forget *slaps*? When Gen Z says something *slaps,* they aren't talking about a physical act of slapping. No, they're talking about something that's really good, especially when it comes to music. "This new song is fire, it totally slaps!" In the Gen Z world, *fire* is also a common term for something that's great or exciting, adding to their colorful lexicon.

If you think Gen Z is confusing, just wait until you meet Gen Alpha (born after 2013). This generation is growing up in an even more tech-saturated world. Gen Alpha has been exposed to everything from virtual reality (VR) to artificial intelligence (AI) from an early age. Although they have inherited much of the slang from Gen Z, they've also introduced their own spin on things. Consider the term "rizz," for example. A shorthand for "charisma," this word is commonly used by Gen Alpha to describe an individual's effortless ability to attract or charm others. "He's got the rizz," could be a way of saying someone has great charm or appeal. Even, the Oxford University Press named "rizz" the 2023 Word of the Year, recognizing its widespread use in describing someone's charisma or charm. Another popular term is *aura*, which refers to the energy or vibe that a person gives off. Someone with a "good aura" might be seen as someone with positive, calming energy. And if you've ever heard the phrase *"Thank you, Beyoncé,"* you might be confused at first. Gen Z and Alpha use it to express gratitude or admiration, often in an exaggerated, humorous way. For instance, after a friend does something impressive, you might exclaim, "Thank you, Beyoncé!" as a playful way of acknowledging their skills or talent. In addition to these, Gen Alpha is known for quickly adopting trends from social media platforms like TikTok, Snapchat, and Instagram, where abbreviations like "FYP" (For You Page) and *no cap* (no lie) are frequently used to convey excitement or emphasis in a conversation.

The year 2025 heralds the arrival of Generation Beta, encompassing individuals born from 2025 to 2039. This generation will experience a seamless integration of digital and physical realms, with artificial intelligence and automation deeply embedded in all aspects of life, including education, work, healthcare, and entertainment. They are likely to be pioneers in using autonomous transportation, wearable health technologies, and immersive virtual environments as everyday norms. Personalization will play a significant role in their upbringing, as AI algorithms will tailor their learning experiences, shopping preferences, and social interactions in unprecedented ways. As Generation Beta emerges, language is expected to evolve rapidly, reflecting their unique experiences and the seamless integration of technology in their lives. With the prevalence of AI and personalized communication, new terms and expressions will likely arise that emphasize brevity and clarity, further shaping how they interact in both digital and physical spaces. This generation will continue the trend of creating a dynamic lexicon that mirrors their fast-paced environment, making language more fluid and adaptable than ever before.

Why Understanding Gen Z/Alpha Slang is Essential?

Learning Gen Z and Alpha slang is not just a trend; it's an essential skill for anyone looking to communicate effectively with these generations. Whether you are an educator, a parent, or a professional, understanding the language of today's youth can help bridge the gap between generations and create more meaningful connections. The language used by Gen Z and Alpha reflects their unique values, preferences, and their need for speed in communication. With the rise of digital technologies, social media, and the fast-paced nature of their daily lives, these generations have developed a lexicon that allows them to convey complex ideas in a fraction of the time it would take to do so traditionally.

One of the key characteristics of Gen Z and Alpha slang is its emphasis on brevity. These generations are accustomed to having vast amounts of information at their fingertips and have developed a language that mirrors this reality. Acronyms, abbreviations, and slang terms like *NSFW* (Not Safe for Work), *iykyk* (If You Know, You Know), *IDK* (I Don't Know), and *sus* (suspicious) allow them to communicate entire concepts with just a few words. This need for speed is deeply ingrained in how they process and shares information.

Educators need to grasp that language goes beyond vocabulary—it encompasses the very fabric of a generation's identity. By learning Gen Z and Alpha slang, educators gain insight into how these students view the world, how they relate to others, and what matters most to them. For instance, slang terms like *rizz* (charm or ability to flirt) have not only entered their conversations but have also started to gain recognition in mainstream culture. In fact, *rizz* was named *Word of the Year* by Oxford University Press in 2023, a clear indication of how these words are evolving from casual speech to part of the broader cultural lexicon. This is an example of how language can evolve quickly, and why it is so important for educators to keep up. Terms that once started in niche online spaces are now becoming part of daily communication, even in professional and social settings.

The impact of Gen Z and Alpha slang extends far beyond the classroom or personal interactions. These words and phrases are gradually being incorporated into mainstream advertising, marketing campaigns, and even content aimed at older generations. As businesses, media outlets, and influencers recognize the influence of this new generation, they too begin using these terms to connect with younger audiences. When a brand uses phrases like *"That's lit"* or *"No cap"* in its advertising, it's not just trying to sound cool—it's trying to build rapport with a generation that values authenticity and relatability. These words speak to the interests, cultural influences, and attitudes of Gen Z and Alpha, allowing brands to tap into their world in a way that feels genuine.

Popular YouTube channels and media platforms have hosted interactive quizzes and interviews featuring global dignitaries and celebrities to test their knowledge of Gen Z/Alpha slang. Videos like these often go viral, garnering millions of views as audiences find it entertaining to see well-respected figures navigate terms like *"rizz," "no cap,"* and *"slaps."* These interactive quizzes, which often gauge how "up-to-date" someone is with Gen Z/Alpha language, highlight just how deeply embedded this language is in contemporary culture. This reflects how language has become a cultural currency, where understanding the trends is not just about knowing the words but also staying in tune with the values and mindset of the generations that shape them.

For educators, parents, and public figures like politicians and celebrities, the integration of Gen Z and Alpha slang into mainstream culture should be seen as a call to action. Understanding and engaging with this language allows them to build stronger connections with younger generations and communicate in a way that resonates with their experiences and cultural touchstones. For example, a principal at a graduation ceremony saying, *"This year's valedictorian has some serious rizz—no cap!"* can inject humor and relatability into a formal setting. Similarly, a politician at a youth rally attempting to connect with the crowd might say, *"Your energy today? It's giving inspiration!"* or a celebrity on a talk show praising a co-star could comment, *"Their acting skills in the movie? Pure rizzler vibes— fr, no cap!"* These phrases are far more than playful words; they reflect an understanding of the younger generation's world and, in turn, help foster trust, relatability, and engagement. By incorporating this language thoughtfully, educators, parents, and public figures can create environments—whether in classrooms, homes, or public platforms—where young people feel seen, heard, and understood.

Language serves as a window into their culture, preferences, and thought processes. By understanding Gen Z or Gen

Alpha language, educators, parents, and professionals can bridge the generational divide, gaining valuable insight into the values, preferences, and experiences of today's youth. Slang is an evolving and dynamic form of communication, one that offers a window into the unique perspectives of younger generations. In a world that is increasingly interconnected and digital, staying fluent in Gen Z and Alpha's language is key to building better relationships, fostering understanding, and creating a more inclusive and engaging world for everyone.

Illustration of Gen Z/Alpha in Conversation

Twin, this guy got mad motion
Fr bro he is a rizzler

Okay, so 'no cap' means I'm not lying or exaggerating
Wait, so if I say, Your explanation is fire, 'no cap,' does that make sense?
Exactly! Now you're vibing, Miss!

?
"Yo, squad, no L's today, we're built different. Stay locked in, push for the W"

bro, why you acting so sus
Chill, I was just goofing around

Why are you two always on your phones? Back in my day, we didn't need any of this technology.
Yeah, fr. We're scrolling for memes lowkey self-care, you know?
Relax, gramps, we're just vibin'. It ain't that serious.

How was your picnic?
Mom, it was lit! Lunch was bussin'.. I fanumtaxed Jake's lunch and received 100+ aura ...no cap

Glossary of
Gen Z/Alpha Words

GEN Z/ALPHA WORDS

A and B the C of D (Above and Beyond the Call of Duty) – An expression meaning something that is exceptional or very good, surpassing normal expectations.
Example: Her performance on the project was truly a and b the c of d."

Addy (/ˈædi/) – A casual shorthand for "address," typically used when asking for someone's location or personal details.
Example: "Can you send me your addy so I can send the package?"

Adulting (/əˈdʌltɪŋ/) – Taking on adult responsibilities and tasks.
Example: "I'm adulting today, paying bills and doing laundry."

Ag (/æg/) – Short for "aggression." Often used to describe someone acting confrontational or showing an intense attitude.
Example: "Why's he coming at me with so much ag?"

Aimée (/ˈeɪmeɪ/) – A term used to describe a girl who is not only beautiful but also kind-hearted, funny, and often

humble about her own beauty. She tends to downplay her attractiveness, but anyone who spends time with her quickly notices her charm and inner beauty.
Example: "Aimée is always making everyone laugh with her jokes, and she doesn't even realize how stunning she is."

Alfie (/ˈæl.fi/) – A nickname or term used to refer to someone who's cool or charming, often used ironically in pop culture.
Example: "You're looking so Alfie today with those sunglasses."

All In (/ɔːl ɪn/) – Fully committed to something or someone.
Example: "He's all in on this new video game."

Alpha (/ˈæl.fə/) – Often used to refer to someone who is seen as a leader, confident, or dominant in a group. It can also refer to the first or best of something, like the "alpha" version of a product.
Example: "He's always the alpha in our friend group."

Amped (/æmpt/) – Full of energy or excitement.
Example: "I'm so amped for the concert tonight!"

Artsy (/ˈɑrt.si/) – Refers to something or someone creative, artistic, or stylish.
Example: "Her Instagram is so artsy, look at all the cool photos."

Ate (/eɪt/) – Slang for performing exceptionally well, particularly in a social, creative, or competitive setting. Often used to hype someone up or praise their efforts.
Example: "Her dance performance was insane—she ate and left the audience speechless!"

Ate and left no crumbs (/eɪt ænd lɛft noʊ krʌmz/) – Describes someone who performed so exceptionally well that there's no room for improvement or competition.
Example: "Did you see Emma's floor routine? She ate and left no crumbs!"

Average day in Ohio (/ˈævərɪdʒ deɪ ɪn oʊˈhaɪoʊ/) – A phrase used to describe something bizarre, unexpected, or chaotic, often with a humorous or ironic tone. Stems from internet memes that depict Ohio as a place of strange occurrences.
Example: "Did you see that guy riding a unicycle with a raccoon on his shoulder? Just an average day in Ohio!"

Auro (/ˈɔːroʊ/) – Overall vibe or energy.
Example: "Her auro is so positive, everyone loves being around her."

Axolotl (/ˌæksəˈlɒtl/) – Referring to the cute amphibian, often used in memes or as a quirky expression to describe something or someone unique or unexpected.
Example: "You're like an axolotl, you're so cute and unique!"

B

Bae (/beɪ/) – A term of endearment for a significant other, short for "before anyone else"
Example: "I'm going to the movies with my bae tonight."

Baddie (/ˈbæd.i/) – A term used to describe someone, usually a woman, who is confident, attractive, and stylish.
Example: "Look at her outfit and that confidence—she's a total baddie!"

Balenciaga (/bæˌlɛn.siˈɑːgə/) – Referring to the high-fashion brand, it's often used as shorthand for anything luxurious or high-end.
Example: "Those shoes are straight-up Balenciaga, wow!"

Banger (/ˈbæŋ.ər/) – Refers to something that is really good, particularly used for music or events that are energetic and exciting.
Example: "That new track is a banger!"

Babymooning (/ˈbeɪ.biˌmuː.nɪŋ/) – Taking a break or vacation right before a big life change, such as a wedding or having a baby.
Example: "They're babymooning in the Maldives before the baby arrives."

Basic (/ˈbeɪ.sɪk/) – Refers to a person who is considered unoriginal or overly conventional, often following mainstream trends and fashions without much individuality.
Example: "I'm not trying to be basic, but I really do love pumpkin spice lattes."

Beef (/biːf/) – Slang for a disagreement, conflict, or feud between two individuals or groups.

Example: "Did you hear about the beef between those two rappers? It's getting serious."

Benching (/ˈbɛn.tʃɪŋ/) – The act of keeping someone on standby, typically in a romantic context, by giving them attention sporadically without fully committing or investing in the relationship.

Example: "I thought we were getting close, but now I realize he's just benching me – texting me occasionally, but never making real plans."

Beyoncé (/beɪˈɒnseɪ/) – Refers to someone who is exceptionally talented, confident, or admired, often used to describe a woman who embodies empowerment and success. It's also used to indicate a high standard of excellence or fame, much like the pop icon herself.
Example: "She walked into the room like she was Beyoncé—everyone was in awe!"

Big Man (/bɪg mæn/) – Refers to someone who is confident, respected, and often a leader in a social setting. It can be used sincerely to acknowledge someone's importance or ironically to tease someone acting overly self-important.
Example: "Oh, look who's calling the shots now—Big Man over here!"

Big Mood (/bɪg muːd/) – Used to express strong relatability to a situation or feeling. It's often used when someone agrees with an emotion or attitude that someone else has expressed, emphasizing how much they share the same sentiment.

Big Yikes (/bɪg ˈjaɪks/) – Used when something is so embarrassing or awkward that a simple "yikes" isn't enough to express the level of discomfort or cringe.
Example: "She tripped in front of the entire class, big yikes!"

Blud (/blʌd/) – A term used for a close friend or mate.
Example: "What's up, blud? How have you been?"

Bombaclat (/ˈbɒm.bəˌklæt/) – A term originating in Jamaican Patois, often used as an exclamation to express surprise, frustration, or disbelief.
Example: "Bombaclat! Did you really just eat the whole pizza by yourself?"

Boomer (/ˈbuː.mər/) – Originally referring to someone from the Baby Boomer generation, it is now used as a term to describe someone who is out of touch with modern trends or technology.
Example: "Stop acting like such a boomer, get with the times!"

Bop (/bɒp/) – A term used to describe a catchy or good song.
Example: "This new song is a total bop, I can't stop playing it."

Boss Up (/bɒs ʌp/) – To level up in terms of confidence, success, or personal growth.
Example: "She bossed up this year, got a promotion, and bought her dream car."

Boujee (/ˈbuː.ʒi/) – Refers to someone or something that is luxurious or expensive, often with a focus on high status or materialism.

Example: "She's so boujee, always wearing designer clothes."

Brainrot (/ˈbreɪnˌrɒt/) – Used to describe the feeling of being overly obsessed with something to the point that it occupies your thoughts constantly.

Example: "I've been watching this show nonstop—it's giving me brainrot."

Budging (/ˈbʌdʒɪŋ/) – To move or shift, but in slang, it often refers to someone being unwilling to change their position or opinion, typically used to describe stubbornness or a refusal to compromise.
Example: "She's not budging on the plans, she insists we go to that restaurant."

Bussin' (/ˈbʌs.ɪn/) – A quirky word to describe something that tastes amazing or is really good, often used when referring to food.
Example: "This pizza is bussin'! You have to try it."

Breadcrumbing (/ˈbredˌkrʌm.ɪŋ/) – Sending intermittent, non-committal messages to someone to maintain their interest without any intention of pursuing a serious relationship.
Example: "He keeps texting me every few days, but it's just breadcrumbing – no real plans to hang out."

Beerboarding (/ˈbɪrˌbɔːr.dɪŋ/) – A playful or humorous term referring to the act of aggressively encouraging or pressuring someone to drink beer, often in a competitive or social context.
Example: "He tried to avoid it, but his friends kept beerboarding him until he gave in."

Bye Felicia (/baɪ fəˈliːʃə/) – A dismissive phrase used to indicate that someone is leaving or being dismissed without much concern or care.
Example: "You're complaining again? Bye Felicia!"

C

Camp (/kæmp/) – Refers to something that is ironically trendy or intentionally exaggerated in style.
Example: "That outfit is so camp, I love it—it's like the ultimate in exaggerated fashion!"

Cap (/kæp/) – A lie or falsehood.
Example: "He said he met Billie Eilish? Cap!"

Capisce (/kəˈpiːʃ/) – Used to confirm understanding, often humorously or informally.
Example: "You need to finish your chores before going out, capisce?"

Capitol (/ˈkæp.ɪ.təl/) – Used to describe something or someone that is extreme, over-the-top, or exaggerated, typically in a funny or dramatic way.
Example: "That drama is capitol! They really took it to the next level."

CEO (/siːˈoʊ/) – Used to describe someone who is highly skilled, competent, or exceptional at something.
Example: "Did you see her crush that presentation? She's the CEO of public speaking!"

Chad Alpha (/tʃæd ˈæl.fə/) – A term used to describe a strong, attractive, and masculine man.
Example: "He's the Chad Alpha of the group—always the center of attention and the one everyone looks up to."

Cheugy (/ˈtʃuː.gi/) – Out of date, trying too hard to be cool
Example: "Those skinny jeans are so cheugy."

Chillaxation (/tʃɪˌlæksˈeɪ.ʃən/) – A blend of "chill" and "relaxation," referring to the art of chilling out in a very relaxed way.
Example: "This weekend is all about chillaxation—no plans, just lounging around."

Clout (/klaʊt/) – Influence or fame.
Example: "She only hangs out with them for the clout."

Colombusing (/kəˈlʌm.bəs.ɪŋ/) – Discovering something that already exists, especially when someone claims credit for it.
Example: "Stop Colombusing – we've been using that app for months, and now you're acting like you found it first!"

Clutch (/klʌtʃ/) – Refers to something that is done at the last minute or when needed the most, often with great success.
Example: "That last-minute save was clutch! We wouldn't have won without it."

Cringe (/krɪndʒ/) – Something awkward or embarrassing.
Example: "That video was so cringe, I couldn't watch it."

Curve (/kɜrv/) – To reject someone or avoid them.
Example: "I tried texting him, but he curved me."

Couch-Potato (/kaʊtʃ pəˈteɪ.toʊ/) – The act of staying on the couch all day, indulging in relaxation.
Example: "I spent the whole Sunday couch-potatoing and watching old reruns."

Cuffing (/ˈkʌf.ɪŋ/) – The act of entering into a committed relationship during the colder months.
Example: "I always see people cuffing in the fall, but by spring, they've usually broken up."

Cuffing Season (/ˈkʌf.ɪŋ ˈsiː.zən/) – The time of year when people search for a relationship.
Example: "It's cuffing season, everyone's looking for a boo."

Catch Feelings (/kætʃ ˈfiː.lɪŋz/) – To develop romantic feelings for someone.
Example: "I didn't mean to catch feelings, but here we are."

D

Dab (/dæb/) – A dance move where a person drops their head into the crook of one arm while raising the other arm outward, often used to express excitement or confidence.
Example: "He hit the *dab* after scoring the game-winning shot!"

Dabbed Out (/dæbd aʊt/) – A term used to describe someone who is overly enthusiastic or shows excessive confidence, especially in social situations.
Example: "She walked into the party, and she was totally *dabbed out* in her new outfit."

Dank (/dæŋk/) – High-quality or cool.
Example: "This meme is *dank*!"

Dart (/dɑːrt/) – Refers to quickly leaving a place or situation, usually in a sneaky or unannounced manner.
Example: "She just darted out of the party before anyone noticed."

Dayumm (/deɪəm/) – An expression of strong approval, admiration, or surprise, often used to react to something impressive or shocking.
Example: "*Dayumm*, that new car is looking fire!"

Deadass (/ˈdɛdˌæs/) – Used to emphasize that something is true or serious.
Example: "I'm *deadass* tired, I need to sleep."

Defenestrate (/ˌdɛfəˈnɛstreɪt/) – To throw someone or something out of a window, often used figuratively to describe the act of removing something dramatically.
Example: "After the meeting, I just wanted to *defenestrate* all those reports—they were completely useless!"

Delulu (/dəˈluːluː/) – A term used to describe someone who is in denial or living in a fantasy world.
Example: "She thinks he's going to text her back, but girl, you're being *delulu*."

Dizzying (/ˈdɪziɪŋ/) – Refers to something that is overwhelming or confusing, often used to describe emotions, events, or experiences.
Example: "The amount of information in that meeting was dizzying."

Doomscrolling (/ˈduːmˌskroʊ.lɪŋ/) – The act of endlessly scrolling through negative news or social media.
Example: "I spent the whole night *doomscrolling* and now I'm stressed."

Dog Water (/dɔːg ˈwɔːtər/) – Something of extremely poor quality or when someone does something poorly.
Example: "That movie was *dog water*, I can't believe I wasted two hours on that."

Don't Do Me Dirty (/doʊnt du mi ˈdɜːr.ti/) – Used when someone feels wronged by another person's actions.
Example: "I helped you out when you needed it, so *don't do me dirty* by lying to me now."

Dope (/doʊp/) – Cool, awesome, or impressive.
Example: "That new song is *dope!*"

Drop (/drɑp/) – To release something, often used for music or products.
Example: "The new album is *dropping* tomorrow."

Drip (/drɪp/) – Refers to a person's style, particularly their clothes and accessories.
Example: "His *drip* is on point today!"

Doxxing (/ˈdɑks.ɪŋ/) – Publicly revealing private information about someone without consent, often maliciously.
Example: "They were accused of *doxxing* a celebrity online."

Delusionship (/dɪˈluː.ʒənʃɪp/) – A term used to describe a relationship that is unrealistic or based on delusions.
Example: "Their relationship is a total *delusionship*—everything looks perfect on social media, but it's a mess in real life."

Drunk Texting (/drʌŋk ˈtɛkst.ɪŋ/) – Sending texts to someone while under the influence of alcohol.
Example: "I accidentally sent a *drunk text* to my ex last night."

Dumbflex (/dʌmˈflɛks/) – A display of something unnecessarily extravagant or showy that seems unintelligent or boastful.
Example: "He just posted a *dumbflex* showing off his new car, even though no one asked."

Eat (/it/) – To perform or do something excellently, especially in reference to someone's skills or actions.
Example: "Did you see that rap battle? She totally ate it."

Elder Millennial (/ˈɛldər mɪˈlɛnɪəl/) – A term for people born on the cusp of Generation X and Millennial generations, usually between the early '80s and mid-'90s.
Example: "As an elder millennial, I get all the memes about dial-up internet and VHS tapes."

Electric (/ɪˈlɛktrɪk/) – Describes something that is highly energetic, exciting, or thrilling.
Example: "The atmosphere at the concert was electric—everyone was dancing."

E-girl / E-boy (/iː gɜrl/ /iː bɔɪ/) – A style or aesthetic associated with emo, goth, and alternative fashion, often seen on TikTok and Instagram.
Example: "He's such an e-boy with all those chains and dyed hair."

Emo (/ˈiː.moʊ/) – Describes a subculture that revolves around emotional expression and alternative music, but it's also used to describe someone being overly emotional or dramatic.
Example: "Stop being so emo and just tell me what happened."

Epstein (/ˈɛpˌstiːn/) – A term that has become shorthand in popular culture, primarily associated with Jeffrey Epstein, often invoked in discussions of wealth, power, exploitation, and conspiracy theories.

Example: "Ever since the Epstein case blew up, people have been questioning the connections between the rich and powerful."

Epic (/ˈɛp.ɪk/) – Used to describe something that is amazing, extraordinary, or impressive.
Example: "That party was epic, we had the best time."

Errand Boy (/ˈɛrənd bɔɪ/) – Used to describe someone who is used by others to do menial tasks or favors, often in a demeaning way.
Example: "Stop being an errand boy for him—he's just using you."

Euphoria (/juːˈfɔːrɪə/) – Refers to the intense feeling of excitement or happiness, especially associated with the TV show *Euphoria*.
Example: "That concert gave me total euphoria, I never want it to end."

Extra (/ˈɛk.strə/) – Refers to someone who is over the top or does more than necessary.
Example: "She was being extra with her outfit today—like, why the sunglasses inside?"

Fam (/fæm/) – Short for family, used to refer to close friends or people you feel connected to.
Example: "I'm hanging with my fam this weekend."

Famalam (/ˈfæm.ə.læm/) – A playful term for a close group of friends or chosen family.
Example: "I'm hanging out with the famalam this weekend!"

Fanum Tax (/ˈfæ.nəm tæks/) – A playful term used to describe the act of "stealing" or taking food from a friend's plate or stash without asking, often as part of friendly banter.
Example: "Yo, stop taking my fries, that's fanum tax!"

Finesse (/fɪˈnɛs/) – To handle a situation skillfully, often with smoothness or charm, sometimes involving trickery.
Example: "He finessed his way into getting free tickets."

Finna (/ˈfɪn.ə/) – A variation of "fixing to," used to express the intent to do something soon.
Example: "I'm finna head out, are you coming?"

Finstas (/ˈfɪn.stəz/) – Refers to "fake Instagram" accounts, usually a secondary account for more personal or unfiltered content shared with close friends.
Example: "She only posts on her finsta when she's with her besties."

Flex (/flɛks/) – To show off, especially in an excessive way.
Example: "She's always flexing her new sneakers on Instagram."

Food Baby (/fuːd ˈbeɪ.bi/) – The bloated feeling after overeating, often resembling a "baby bump."
Example: "I'm lying down now with a food baby after that massive Thanksgiving dinner."

Flexting (/ˈflɛks.tɪŋ/) – Showing off or bragging on social media to impress a love interest, often by posting gym selfies, travel pictures, or content tailored to their interests.
Example: "He's been flexting hard with those book reviews ever since he found out she's into literature."

Flipped (/flɪpt/) – Refers to a dramatic change in someone's mood, attitude, or situation.
Example: "She flipped when she saw her surprise birthday party."

Fly (/flaɪ/) – Used to describe something or someone that looks stylish, impressive, or fashionable.
Example: "Those shoes are fly, where did you get them?"

FR (For Real) (/fɔr riːl/) – Used to emphasize sincerity or agreement with something, often to confirm that someone isn't joking.
Example: "That test was tough, FR."

Fire (/ˈfaɪər/) – Used to describe something that is extremely good, exciting, or impressive.
Example: "That new song is fire!"

G

Gassed (/gæst/) – Feeling hyped or overly confident about something.
Example: "He was so gassed after winning the game."

Gassed Up (/gæst ʌp/) – To be overly excited or hyped about something.
Example: "She's so gassed up about her new outfit."

Geeked out (/giːkt aʊt/) – To become extremely excited, enthusiastic, or obsessed about something, often related to a particular hobby or interest.
Example: "I totally geeked out when I saw the new Star Wars trailer!"

Ghosting (/ˈɡoʊstɪŋ/) – Suddenly cutting off communication with someone without any explanation.
Example: "He just ghosted me after I texted him."

Ghostlighting (/ˈɡoʊstˌlaɪtɪŋ/) – A combination of ghosting (disappearing from someone's life) and gaslighting (manipulating someone's perception of reality).
Example: "He started ghostlighting me—pretending nothing happened while making me doubt myself."

Glizzy (/ˈɡlɪzi/) – A hotdog or, in some cases, a slang term for a gun.
Example: "I can't wait to eat this glizzy at the cookout."

Glow Up (/gloʊ ʌp/) – A noticeable transformation or improvement in appearance, style, or success.
Example: "She had a major glow up after she moved to New York."

Glowed Up (/gloʊd ʌp/) – To undergo a transformation, especially regarding appearance.
Example: "He really glowed up after high school."

Goofed (/guːft/) – To make a mistake or mess up in a funny or clumsy way.
Example: "I goofed and sent the message to the wrong person!"

Go Off (/goʊ ɔf/) – To express strong emotions or to do something confidently.
Example: "She went off on the teacher after the unfair grade."

Guap (/gwɑp/) – A slang term for a large amount of money.
Example: "He made a lot of guap from his online business."

Gurl (/gɜrl/) – A playful or exaggerated way of saying "girl," often used for emphasis or humor.
Example: "Gurl, you need to try this new lipstick shade."

Get the Bag (/gɛt ðə bæg/) – To earn money, typically by hustling or working hard.
Example: "He's working on his side business to get the bag."

GUCCI (/ˈguː.tʃi/) – Used to describe something that is good, cool, fashionable, or excellent.
Example: "That new jacket you bought? It's so Gucci!"

Gyatt/Gyat (/gaɪæt/) – A slang term used to express strong excitement, surprise, or admiration.
Example: "Did you see her outfit? Gyatt, she looks amazing!"

Hangry (/ˈhæŋgri/) – A blend of "hungry" and "angry," describing irritability from being very hungry.
Example: "I'm so hangry, I need to eat something right now!"

Headass (/ˈhɛdˌæs/) – A playful insult for someone acting dumb, clueless, or silly in a bad way.
Example: "You're acting like a headass right now, just stop."

He/She belongs to the streets (/hiː/ʃi brˈlɔŋz tu ðə strits/) – Used to imply that someone is uncommitted, disloyal, or promiscuous.
Example: "He's out every night with a new crowd—he's definitely for the streets."

Hella (/ˈhɛlə/) – Informal term meaning "a lot" or "very," used to emphasize quantity or intensity.
Example: "I have hella homework tonight."

High Key (/haɪ ki/) – Used to describe something obvious or openly stated, as opposed to "low key."
Example: "I'm high key obsessed with this new album."

Hits Different (/hɪts 'dɪfərənt/) – Describes something that has a deeper or more significant impact than expected.
Example: "This pizza hits different after a long day."

Hiberdating (/'haɪbərˌdeɪtɪŋ/) – Describes withdrawing from social activities to focus on staying at home, resting, or being cozy.
Example: "I've been hiberdating all weekend—just me, my blanket, and Netflix."

Hive Mind (/haɪv maɪnd/) – Refers to a group of people thinking and acting collectively.
Example: "The internet has become a hive mind when it comes to this new trend."

Hoe (/hoʊ/) – Someone who only seeks casual relationships with no emotional depth, often prioritizing sex and money.
Example: "He's not interested in anything serious, just jumping from one hookup to the next—total hoe behavior."

Hold This L (/hoʊld ðɪs ɛl/) – To accept defeat or acknowledge failure, often in a humorous or taunting manner.
Example: "You lost the game? Hold this L!"

Horthetic (/hɔːrˈθɛtɪk/) – Something so pathetic or embarrassing that it's hard to describe.
Example: "His attempt at dancing was so horthetic, I had to look away."

Hundo P (/ˈhʌndoʊ pi/) – Short for "100 percent," expressing full agreement or certainty.
Example: "I'm hundo P sure I want to go to that concert."

Huggy (/ˈhʌgi/) – Describes something or someone that is sweet, affectionate, or cuddly.
Example: "That new puppy is so huggy, I just want to hold him all day."

Huzz (/hʌz/) – A term used to show excitement, agreement, or to hype up a situation or person. Often used in celebratory contexts or to cheer someone on.
Example: "Huzz! We finally won the game!"

I

I'm Baby (/aɪm ˈbeɪbi/) – Used to express vulnerability or innocence, often in a self-deprecating or playful way. It's a way of saying that you're feeling overwhelmed, need comfort, or aren't fully equipped to handle something challenging.

I oop (/aɪ uːp/) – Used to express shock, surprise, or embarrassment, often in response to something unexpected or awkward.
Example: "I accidentally spilled my drink on him—I oop."

Iced Out (/aɪst aʊt/) – An adjective used to describe a piece of jewelry or accessory that is heavily adorned with diamonds or other shiny gems, often in an ostentatious display of wealth. It can also be associated with showing off material success, typically linked to street culture or the hip-hop community.
Example: "Look at that chain—he's totally iced out with diamonds all over it."

India is not for beginners (/ˈɪndiə ɪz nɒt fɔː bɪˈɡɪnəz/) – This phrase is used humorously or sarcastically to suggest that a situation, person, or place is complex, intense, or challenging, often requiring experience, resilience, or savvy to navigate successfully. It implies that something may be overwhelming for "beginners" or those without prior exposure.
Example: Learning Crypto trading? Bruh! India is not for beginners."

Oompfh (/ʊm.f/) – Used to describe a feeling of impact, energy, or intensity, often in a physical or emotional context. It conveys something that has a powerful or impressive effect, like a burst of excitement or strength.
Example: "That performance had so much oompfh, I couldn't stop watching!"

iPad kid (/ˈaɪpæd kɪd/) – A derogatory term for Generation Alpha children who spend a lot of time in front of screens, especially on devices like iPads, often viewed critically.
Example: "My younger cousin is such an iPad kid, she can't stay off her tablet for a minute."

Issa Vibe (/ˈɪsə vaɪb/) – Used to describe something that gives off a positive or enjoyable feeling. Often used to describe a situation, mood, or person that is particularly chill or good.
Example "That party last night? Issa vibe."

It's giving (/ɪts ˈgɪvɪŋ/) – Used to describe the vibe, impression, or overall attitude that someone or something conveys, often positively or admiringly.
Example: "That new song is giving me summer vibes!"

Jacked (/dʒækt/) – Used to describe someone who is very muscular or in great physical shape.

Example: "Look at him, he's totally jacked!"

J-Cole Debate (/'dʒeɪ koʊl dɪ'beɪt/) – A debate where one side is obviously wrong, but continues anyway, despite being totally illogical or ignorant.

Example: "Don't bother arguing with her, it's just a J-Cole Debate."

Janky (/ˈdʒæŋki/) – Refers to something that is poorly made, subpar, or of low quality. It can describe anything from technology to people's behavior.
Example: "This phone is so janky, it barely works."

Jelly (/ˈdʒɛli/) – Short for "jealous." Used to express envy or feeling jealous about something someone else has or is doing.
Example: "I'm so jelly of her new shoes!"

Jit (/dʒɪt/) – A term used to describe a person, usually a younger or inexperienced one.
Example: "Don't listen to him, he's just a jit."

Jive (/dʒaɪv/) – To go along with something or agree. It can also refer to the feeling of rhythm or flow in music.
Example: "That vibe really jives with me.

Juiced (/dʒuːst/) – Feeling excited or hyped about something. Often used to describe high energy or enthusiasm toward an event or activity.
Example: "I'm juiced for the concert this weekend!"

Karen (/ˈkærən/) – A demeaning term referring to a white middle-aged woman who acts in an unreasonable, rude, petty, or entitled manner, often expecting special treatment or causing unnecessary conflict.
Example: "Just let it go, it's not worth it. Don't be such a Karen."

Kardashian Effect (/kɑːˈdæʃən ɪˈfɛkt/) – Refers to someone who is always in the spotlight, often associated with influencers or celebrities who maintain a constant media presence.
Example: "She's got that Kardashian effect, always posting and getting noticed."

Keep it 100 (/kiːp ɪt wʌn ˈhʌndrəd/) – To be completely honest, real, or authentic. Refers to staying true to oneself and always being honest.
Example: "I'm just keeping it 100 with you, that movie was terrible."

Kiki (/ˈkiːki/) – A term used to describe a fun, carefree gathering, often among close friends, associated with laughing, gossiping, or just having a good time.
Example: "We had such a great kiki last night, just talking and laughing the whole time."

Kittenfishing (/ˈkɪtənˌfɪʃɪŋ/) – A term used in online dating and social media to describe the act of presenting a misleading or altered version of oneself, often using old or heavily edited photos, in order to appear more attractive or interesting.
Example: "He seemed so much better-looking in his profile photos, but when we met, it was obvious he was kittenfishing."

Knock-off (/ˈnɒkˌɔːf/) – Refers to a product that is a cheap imitation of something original, often used for designer items.
Example: "That's a knock-off bag, not the real deal."

Kween (/kwiːn/) – A playful variation of "queen," used to praise someone, especially a woman, for their strength, confidence, or fabulousness.
Example: "You're such a kween, slaying that outfit!"

Karma (/ˈkɑːrmə/) – The belief that a person's actions, whether good or bad, will eventually come back to them.
Example: "Don't mess with her, she's got some serious karma coming her way."

Kale (/keɪl/) – Refers to something that is trendy, cool, or fashionable, especially in the context of health and wellness.
Example: "That kale smoothie you made is so healthy and fresh."

Keg Stand (/kɛg stænd/) – A party trick where someone does a handstand on top of a keg, often used in college or party settings.
Example: "I dare you to do a keg stand at the party tonight!"

K-pop Stans (/keɪ ˈpɑːp stænz/) – Refers to the dedicated and passionate fanbase of K-pop (Korean pop) music, known for their loyalty and enthusiasm.
Example: "The K-pop stans are going wild over the new album release!"

Kaleidoscope Eyes (/kəˈlaɪdəˌskoʊp aɪz/) – Describes someone whose eyes have a mesmerizing or multi-dimensional quality, often used for someone whose personality or gaze seems captivating or deep.
Example: "She has kaleidoscope eyes that draw everyone in."

L

L (/ɛl/) – Loss or failure, often used to describe an unfortunate situation.
Example: "I missed the train, big L for me today."

Lit (/lɪt/) – Used to describe something exciting, fun, or high-energy. It can also mean something is really good or excellent.
Example: "That concert was so lit, I had the best time!"

Litty (/ˈlɪti/) – A variation of "lit," used to describe something even more exciting or intense.
Example: "That party was litty, everyone was dancing all night!"

Lituation (/lɪtʃʊˈeɪʃən/) – A combination of "lit" and "situation," meaning an exciting or fun situation.
Example: "The party last night was a full-on lituation."

Love/Hate (/lʌv heɪt/) – Describes a conflicted feeling of both enjoying and being frustrated by something.
Example: "I love/hate that show. It's so dramatic, but I can't stop watching."

Lurking (/lɜːrkɪŋ/) – Refers to watching someone's social media posts without engaging, such as scrolling without liking or commenting.
Example: "I saw you lurking on my profile last night, why didn't you like my post?"

Loser (/'luːzər/) – Used playfully or insultingly to refer to someone not successful or cool, often in a humorous or teasing manner.

Example: "You forgot your keys again? You're such a loser."

Lush (/lʌʃ/) – Describes something or someone that is elegant, fabulous, or luxurious.

Example: "The spa day was so lush, I didn't want to leave."

Liddy (/ˈlɪdi/) – A variation of "lit," used to describe a fun or exciting situation.

Example: "That game was so liddy, we won and the crowd went wild!"

Lowkey (/loʊkiː/) – Refers to something being done or felt in a subtle or secretive way, often used when downplaying something.

Example: "I lowkey think I'm in love with that song."

Luv (/lʌv/) – A shorthand version of "love," often used affectionately or casually.

Example: "Luv you, can't wait to hang out soon!"

Mandem (/ˈmæn.dɛm/) – A term commonly used in British slang to refer to a group of friends, particularly a close-knit group of males. It's often used in urban settings and can also be used to refer to "the crew" or "the squad."
Example: "Yo, I'm meeting up with the mandem later to grab some food."

Mad ting – Good or remarkable.
Example: "That was a mad ting last night!"

MCE (Main Character Energy) (/meɪn ˈkærɪktər ˈɛnədʒi/) – Refers to someone who acts like the main character in a story, displaying confidence, self-assuredness, or standing out.
Example: "She walked into the room with main character energy."

Mogging (/ˈmɒgɪŋ/) – To be more attractive or have more appeal than others, often in a competitive or boastful sense.
Example: "He's really mogging at the party tonight."

Monkey branching (/ˈmʌŋki ˈbræntʃɪŋ/) – A term used in dating or relationship contexts, referring to someone who jumps from one relationship to another without fully letting go of the previous one, similar to how a monkey swings from branch to branch.
Example: "She's always talking to other people while still with him—classic monkey branching."

Mod S (/mɒd ɛs/) – Short for "Modern Style," often used in the context of fashion, design, or lifestyle to refer to a contemporary or trendy aesthetic. It can describe a clean,

minimalist, or forward-thinking approach to style, whether it's in clothing, interior design, or other elements of culture.
Example: "Her apartment is totally mod S, with sleek furniture and minimal decor."

Mooch (/muːtʃ/) – A person who takes or asks for things without giving anything in return. Often used to describe someone who exploits others' generosity or constantly relies on others to provide for them without reciprocating.
Example: "Tency is the biggest mooch I've ever seen."

Monched (/mɒntʃd/) – Used to describe something or someone that is crushed, defeated, or taken down easily, similar to "slayed" or "owned."
Example: "She monched that test; she aced it without even studying."

Mosh (/mɒʃ/) – To jump, push, or dance aggressively in a group, often at concerts in a mosh pit.
Example: *"The crowd started to mosh as soon as the band started playing."*

Munch (/mʌntʃ/) – A term used to refer to someone who is very attractive or "fine" in the context of romantic attraction.
Example: *"He's a total munch."*

MVP (/ˈɛmˈviːˈpiː/) – Refers to the person or thing that stands out as the best in a situation.
Example: *"You're the MVP for helping me study last night."*

Nerdy (/ˈnɜːdi/) – Describes someone who is very interested in academic or niche hobbies.
Example: "She's so nerdy, always reading books about space."

Nervy (/ˈnɜːrvi/) – Describes someone bold, audacious, or slightly rude in their actions.
Example: "That was a nervy move asking for a raise on the first day."

Nice Try, Diddy (/naɪs traɪ, ˈdɪdi/) – A playful phrase used to acknowledge someone's attempt at doing something, usually in a situation where the effort was unsuccessful or fell short, but still with a hint of humour or admiration.

Noob (/nuːb/) – Refers to someone new to something or lacking experience, often in gaming contexts.
Example: "I'm still a noob at this game, I keep losing."

No Cap (/noʊ kæp/) – Used to emphasise that something is truthful or genuine, meaning no lie or exaggeration.
Example: "That new restaurant is amazing, no cap."

Nodding (/ˈnɒdɪŋ/) – Often used to indicate agreement with someone, like saying "I'm with you."
Example: "I was just nodding the whole time during the meeting."

Noodles (/ˈnuːdəlz/) – Refers to something flimsy, weak, or lacking substance, often used to describe someone indecisive.
Example: "Stop being such a noodle and stand up for yourself."

NPC (/ɛn piː siː/) – Stands for "Non-Player Character," referring to people who follow trends or lack independent thought, often used in gaming.
Example: "Don't be such an NPC, think for yourself!"

Nuke (/nuːk/) – Used to describe something being completely destroyed or overwhelmed, often used in gaming or to emphasise intensity.
Example: "They totally nuked the competition with that last move."

Nuts (/nʌts/) – Used to describe something that is crazy, wild, or hard to believe.
Example: "That party last night was nuts!"

O

OG (/oʊˈdʒiː/) – Short for "Original Gangster," it originally referred to someone or something that is authentic, original, or has been around for a long time, often with a sense of admiration.
Example: "That new album is straight fire, but we all know the OGs like Nas and Jay still set the standard."

Oof (/ʊf/) – Used to express discomfort, surprise, dismay, or sympathy for someone else's pain.
Example: "Oof, that test was brutal!"

Ohio (/oʊˈhaɪoʊ/) – Slang to describe something strange, weird, cringe, or dumb.
Example: "That video was so Ohio, I couldn't stop laughing."

Okay, Boomer (/oʊˈkeɪ ˈbuːmər/) – A dismissive phrase used to mock or disagree with older generations, particularly Baby Boomers.
Example: "You think social media is a phase? Okay, Boomer."

Off the rails (/ɔf ðə reɪlz/) – Refers to something that is no longer under control or has gone in an unexpected direction.
Example: "The party went off the rails when the DJ played the wrong track."

On fleek (/ɒn fliːk/) – Perfectly done, flawless, or on point (often used to describe someone's appearance or style).
Example: "Her makeup is on fleek today."

On the grind (/ɒn ðə graɪnd/) – Refers to working hard or hustling, focusing intensely on something.
Example: "I'm on the grind, trying to finish this project before the deadline."

Oomph (/ʊmf/) – Refers to a quality that makes something more exciting, impressive, or energetic. It can also describe a special effort or energy put into something.
Example: "The singer's performance had so much oomph, the crowd went wild!"

Orbiting (/ˈɔːrbɪtɪŋ/) – The act of maintaining a person's attention through social media interactions (such as liking posts, viewing stories, or commenting), without direct communication or any effort to meet in person. It's a way to keep someone engaged online without making any real commitment or moving the relationship forward.
Example: "After our breakup, he started orbiting me, liking all my photos but never actually talking to me."

Out of pocket (/aʊt əv ˈpɒkɪt/) – Used to describe behavior that is inappropriate or beyond the norm.
Example: "That joke was out of pocket, you can't say stuff like that."

Oozing (/ˈuːzɪŋ/) – Used to describe someone or something exuding a lot of confidence, style, or attractiveness.

Periodt (/ˈpɪə.ri.əd/) – A definitive and emphatic way of ending a statement, often used to stress the finality of a statement or argument, similar to saying "end of discussion."
Example: "I've made my decision, periodt."

PG vibes (/piː-ˈdʒiː vaɪbz/) – A relaxed, non-controversial atmosphere, often used to describe an environment or situation that is safe, chill, and free from conflict or tension.
Example: "The party was all PG vibes, everyone was just hanging out and having a good time."

Piped up (/paɪpt ʌp/) – Refers to getting excited or hyped, often at a party or event.
Example: "The crowd piped up when the DJ dropped that track."

Pluh (/plʌ/) – Used as a conversation stopper when there is nothing left to say, indicating a sense of finality or dismissal.
Example: "And that's how it happened... pluh, no more to say about it."

Play (/pleɪ/) – To flirt or make a move on someone romantically.
Example: "He's trying to play me, but I'm not interested."

Pog (/pɒg/) – Used to describe something exciting, impressive, or worthy of praise. Often used in gaming communities.
Example: "That move was so pog!"

Pookie (/ˈpuːki/) – An endearing nickname for a close friend or lover. It originates from a German term of endearment used in the 1900s and is often used as a pet name.
Example: "You're my little pookie, always making me smile."

Poppin' (/ˈpɒpɪn/) – Refers to something that is really exciting, lively, or popular.
Example: "The club was poppin' last night."

Post Yap Clarity (/poʊst jæp ˈklærɪti/) – The feeling of regret or unease after talking for too long, realizing you've said too much or something awkward.

Pre-game (/priːˈgeɪm/) – To drink or hang out before an event, typically a party or night out.
Example: "Let's pre-game before we hit the club."

Pregret (/ˈpriːgrɛt/) – A term used to describe the feeling of regret before even doing something, often due to anticipating a negative outcome or the consequences of an action. It's the anxious feeling of knowing you might regret something, even though you haven't done it yet.

Example: "I'm already pregretting agreeing to this party tonight. I know I'll be exhausted tomorrow!"

Pull up (/pʊl ʌp/) – To show up or arrive at a location, often unexpectedly.

Example: "We're pulling up to the party in 10 minutes."

Pulling the plug (/ˈpʊlɪŋ ðə plʌg/) – Ending something, whether a relationship, an event, or a project, often prematurely.

Example: "They pulled the plug on the meeting early."

Pushing P (/ˈpʊʃɪŋ piː/) – A phrase popularised by rapper Gunna, meaning to stay true to oneself or to be real, keeping things genuine.

Example: "He's just out here pushing P, always keeping it real."

Q

Q (/kjuː/) – An abbreviation sometimes used for "question," especially when asking someone to clarify or elaborate on something.
Example: "Got a Q for you, do you want to hang out later?"

Quad (/kwɒd/) – The term "The Quad" is used to describe the four generations currently working in the workforce: Baby Boomers, Generation X, Millennials, and the Silent Generation.
Example: "The office is an interesting place with all four generations in the quad bringing different perspectives to the table."

Quiet quit (/ˈkwaɪət kwɪt/) – To disengage or do the bare minimum at work or in a situation without officially leaving, often characterised by not making a fuss or quitting publicly.
Example: "I've been quiet quitting at work; just showing up and doing the least."

Quiet storm (/ˈkwaɪət stɔːm/) – Refers to a situation or person that appears calm but is intense, powerful, or unpredictable beneath the surface.
Example: "Don't let her quiet storm fool you; she's a powerhouse."

Quick flex (/kwɪk flɛks/) – A casual or subtle display of something impressive or showing off, typically done in a nonchalant way.
Example: "I just got a new car, quick flex, but no big deal."

Queen (/kwiːn/) – A term used to refer to a woman or a person with regal qualities, often signifying confidence, authority, and leadership.

Example: "She's such a queen, always owning the room."

Queer (/kwɪə/) – A term used to describe a non-heterosexual orientation, often used as an umbrella term for the LGBTQ+ community. It can also describe something that's offbeat or not fitting the norm.

Example: "He identifies as queer, and he's proud of it."

Quicksilver (/ˈkwɪkˌsɪlvə/) – Describes something or someone that moves incredibly fast or is extremely unpredictable, often used for fast changes or unexpected reactions.
Example: "The vibe at the party shifted quicksilver, one minute it was chill, the next it was wild!"

Quirky (/ˈkwɜː.ki/) – Describes someone who is unconventional or unique in an interesting or charming way, often with a playful or eccentric character.
Example: "I love how quirky she is; she's always doing something unexpected."

Qwoot (/kwut/) – An expression of extreme joy or ecstasy, often used to emphasize excitement or happiness. The number of O's typically indicates the intensity of the enthusiasm.
Example: "Albey is here... QWOOT!"

Rad (/ræd/) – Short for "radical," meaning something that is cool, awesome, or impressive.
Example "That concert was rad, I had an amazing time!"

Rap (/ræp/) – Refers to a style of music that originated in the African-American community, characterised by rhythm and rhyming speech. It can also mean to speak or chat informally.
Example "Let's rap about your weekend plans."

Ratio (/ˈreɪʃioʊ/) – Used when one comment or post gets more replies or likes than another, especially in social media. It can be used to indicate that one opinion or post is more popular than another, often used to imply the original post was wrong or unpopular.
Example "You just got ratioed, bro. More replies than likes on your post."

Red flag (/rɛd flæg/) – A warning sign or indication that something is wrong, especially in relationships or situations.
Example: "He canceled our date last minute? That's a red flag."

Rookie (/ˈrʊki/) – A person who is new or inexperienced at something, often used to describe beginners in sports, work, or any activity.
Example: "He's a rookie at this game, so don't expect him to win right away."

Rooftop (/ˈruːfˌtɒp/) – Refers to high-energy or over-the-top behavior, often seen in parties or celebrations.
Example: "That party was rooftop level, we danced all night."

Roll the dice (/roʊl ðə daɪs/) – Taking a risk or chance in the hope of a favourable outcome.
Example: "I'm going to roll the dice and ask them out, wish me luck!"

RIP bozo (/rɪp ˈboʊzoʊ/) – A dismissive or mocking phrase used to express disdain or make fun of someone, often in response to them failing or making a poor decision.
Example: "He tried to talk smack, but now he's just sitting there with no comeback. RIP bozo."

Rizz (/rɪz/) – Short for charisma, referring to a person's charm or ability to attract others, especially in a romantic context.
Example: "Did you see him talking to her? He's got so much rizz!"

Ratchet (/ˈrætʃɪt/) – Used to describe something that is low-class, tacky, or wild in a negative sense.
Example: "That outfit is so ratchet, it's too much."

Roman Empire (/ˈroʊmən ˈɛmpaɪə/) – Refers to a trend where people, especially men, seem to be obsessed with the greatness and legacy of the Roman Empire. It has become a meme or trend symbolizing a fascination with history or power.
Example: "Every time I ask him what he's thinking about, he says 'the Roman Empire.'"

S

Salty (/ˈsɔːlti/) – Used to describe someone who is bitter, upset, or annoyed about something.
Example: "She's still salty about losing the game."

Sending me (/ˈsɛndɪŋ mi/) – Used to describe a reaction of being amused, shocked, or overwhelmed by something, often something funny or absurd.
Example: "Did you see that meme? It's sending me!"

Shaveducking (/ˈʃeɪvˌdʌk.ɪŋ/) – The uncertainty about whether you're attracted to someone's face or the person themselves, often triggered by how they look with or without facial hair.
Example: "I realized I was shaveducking when I couldn't tell if I liked him or just his beard!"

She fine (/ʃi faɪn/) – Used to describe someone, typically a woman, as being physically attractive or looking good.
Example: "I can't stop looking at her—she fine, for real!"

Sheesh (/ʃiːʃ/) – An exclamation used to express disbelief, amazement, or admiration.
Example: "Sheesh, did you see that dunk? That was crazy!"

Shmoney (/ˈʃmʌni/) – Slang for money, often used to describe wealth or financial success.
Example: "He's all about that shmoney these days, just closed a big deal."

Shook (/ʃʊk/) – Describes someone who is shocked, surprised, or startled.
Example: "I was so shook when I saw the plot twist in that movie."

Sigma (/ˈsɪg.mə/) – A person who follows their own path, prioritizing independence and self-reliance over fitting in with social expectations.
Example: "He's always on his grind, doing his own thing—total Sigma vibes."

Simp (/sɪmp/) – A person, usually a man, who is overly attentive or submissive to someone they are attracted to, often to the point of being excessive or self-deprecating.
Example: "He's such a simp for her, he buys her gifts every day."

Sip tea (/sɪp tiː/) – To mind your own business or listen to gossip, often used in situations of judgment or when you›re not directly involved.
Example: "I was just sipping my tea, enjoying the drama."

Skibidi (/ˈskɪbɪdi/) – A nonsensical or playful term with no inherent meaning. It's used in internet culture as a wacky adjective to describe something as cool, bad, or even dumb, often humorously or exaggeratedly. It gained popularity from the viral "Skibidi Toilet" meme and the "Skibidi" song by the Russian band Little Big.
Example: "That new dance move is so skibidi, I can't stop laughing!"

Skibidi Ohio Rizz (/ˈskɪbɪdi oʊˈhaɪoʊ rɪz/) – Refers to someone who is acting weird or exhibiting strange, cringe-worthy behavior, possibly in a way that tries too hard to be charming or appealing.

Example: "Why are you acting like that? You're really pulling a Skibidi Ohio Rizz right now."

Sksksk (/skɪsksk/) – A term used to convey happiness or laughter, often a form of keysmashing. It originated from Brazilian users on Twitter and became popular with the VSCO girl trend. It's commonly used to express excitement or a lighthearted reaction.

Example: *"I just saw the funniest video, sksksk!"*

Slay (/sleɪ/) – To do something exceptionally well, often used to praise someone's appearance or performance.

Example: "She totally slayed her presentation today."

Slaps (/slæps/) – Refers to something that is really good or impressive, especially used to describe music or a good time.
Example: "That concert was so slaps, I had the best time!"

Sleepdrifting (/ˈslipˌdrɪftɪŋ/) – The act of being on your phone or scrolling in bed until you fall asleep.
Example: "I was sleepdrifting last night and woke up with my phone on my face."

Smoke (/smoʊk/) – Trouble or overwhelming situations.
Example: "I knew I was in the smoke when I forgot my homework at home."

Smoked (/smoʊkt/) – Completely defeated or embarrassed.
Example: "During the game, I got smoked so bad I wanted to rage quit."

Swerve (/swɜːrv/) – To avoid someone or something, typically in a physical or metaphorical sense.
Example: "I had to swerve that awkward conversation with my ex."

Squinny (/ˈswɪni/) – A feeling of awkwardness or discomfort after talking too much, leading to self-consciousness or unease.
Example: "I had a squinny moment after I realized I was ranting for 30 minutes about my favourite TV show, and they looked totally uninterested."

Sus (/sʌs/) – Short for "suspicious" or "suspect," used when something seems shady, off, or untrustworthy.
Example: "That guy is acting really sus, I think he's hiding something."

Stan (/stæn/) – To be an extremely dedicated fan of someone or something. Originated from the Eminem song "Stan."
Example: "I stan her so hard, she's such a talented singer."

Sky Daddy (/skaɪ ˈdædi/) – A humorous or sarcastic slang term for God or a higher deity, often used by younger people in a playful, irreverent way. The term suggests a divine figure who is distant and somewhat comically viewed as a paternal figure in the sky.
Example: "I'll pray to Sky Daddy for a good grade on this test!"

———————✦✦———————

Take a Dub (/teɪk ə dʌb/) – To win or succeed in something. "Dub" is short for "W," which stands for "win."
Example: "We're going to take a dub in this game, I can feel it."

Take the L (/teɪk ðə ɛl/) – To lose or accept defeat, often in a situation that is embarrassing or disappointing.
Example: "I had to take the L when I failed the test."

Tea (/tiː/) – Gossip or juicy information. To "spill the tea" means to share gossip, often about someone or something juicy.
Example: "I heard some crazy tea about what happened at the party last night."

Technoference (/tɛk.nəʊˈfɪərəns/) – The disruption of real-life interactions due to the overuse of technology or devices.
Example: "We had a great conversation, but then the technoference kicked in when his phone kept ringing."

Thank You, Beyoncé (/ˈθæŋk juː, ˈbiːˈɑːnseɪ/) – A phrase used to express gratitude or admiration, often sarcastically, after someone does something impressive or worthy of praise. It's inspired by Beyoncé's reputation for excellence.
Example: "You fixed that car with zero experience? Thank you, Beyoncé, for being a DIY legend!"

Thicc (/θɪk/) – Refers to someone with a curvy, fuller figure, often used to describe someone as attractive due to their body shape.
Example: "She's looking thicc in that outfit!"

Touch Grass (/tʌtʃ græs/) – A phrase used to tell someone to step away from the internet or online space and reconnect with the real world, often when someone is too absorbed in digital spaces.

Example: "You've been arguing about that tweet for hours, dude. Maybe it's time to touch grass."

Trill (/trɪl/) – A combination of "true" and "real," used to describe someone who is authentic or genuine.

Example: "That rapper is so trill, he always keeps it real."

Tune (/tjuːn/) – Used to describe a state of mind or mood, often relating to someone's attitude or how they are feeling in the moment. It can also refer to someone who is in a good or confident mood.
Example: "She's in such a good tune today—nothing can bring her down!"

Turnt (/tɜːrnt/) – Used to describe being excited or hyped up, typically in the context of a party, event, or gathering.
Example: "That concert was so turnt, the crowd was going wild!"

Ubiquitous (/juːˈbɪkwɪtəs/) – Something that is present, appearing, or found everywhere.
Example: "Social media has become ubiquitous in our daily lives."

Ubuntu (/ʊˈbʊntuː/) – A Southern African term that refers to the belief in a universal bond that connects all humanity. It translates to "I am because we are," reflecting a sense of shared humanity, community, and interconnectedness. It emphasises the importance of compassion, kindness, and helping others.
Example: "The community worked together to help those in need, showing true ubuntu in action."

Uncouth (/ʌnˈkuːθ/) – Lacking good manners or refinement, crude.
Example: "His uncouth behavior at the dinner table embarrassed everyone."

Underdog (/ˈʌndər‚dɔg/) – A person or group in a competition that is expected to lose.
Example: "Everyone was rooting for the underdog team to win the championship."

Under the Weather (/ˈʌndər ðə ˈwɛðər/) – A phrase meaning to feel ill or unwell.
Example: "I'm feeling a bit under the weather today, so I'm taking the day off."

Uproarious (/ʌpˈrɔːrɪəs/) – Extremely noisy or full of laughter.
Example: "The audience was uproarious after the comedian's jokes."

Utilitarian (/ˌjuːtɪlɪˈtɛəriən/) – Practical, focusing on functionality over aesthetics.
Example: "The design of the apartment was utilitarian, with minimal decoration but lots of storage."

UwU (/juːˈdʌbljuː/, which sounds like "you double-you.") – A term used to convey happiness, affection, or admiration, often used to express cuteness or joy in a playful, endearing way. It is commonly used in online communities and is associated with a cute or soft expression.
Example: "That puppy's smile is so sweet, UwU!"

Vaulted (/ˈvɔːltɪd/) – Describes something that is extremely rare or valuable, often used for exclusive or limited-edition items.
Example: "That designer jacket is vaulted, only a few people own it."

Vibe (/vaɪb/) – Refers to the overall atmosphere, feeling, or energy of a person, place, or thing.
Example: "The vibe at that concert was incredible!"

Vibe Check (/vaɪb tʃɛk/) – A casual way to assess someone's mood, energy, or attitude, often used to determine if someone is in the right mindset for a situation.
Example: "Let's do a vibe check before we head out—are we all good with the plan?"

Villain Arc (/ˈvɪlən ɑːrk/) – A term describing a personal transformation where someone becomes more selfish, vengeful, or behaves in a morally questionable way, often after being hurt or wronged.
Example: "Since he got that promotion, it's like a full villain arc—he's acting like he owns the place."

Viral (/ˈvaɪrəl/) – Describes something that spreads rapidly and widely on the internet, such as a video, meme, or trend.
Example: "That TikTok video went viral within hours!"

W – Short for "win," often used to indicate that something is a success or someone has achieved something great.
Example: "Getting those concert tickets was a big W."

Wallflower (/ˈwɔːlˌflaʊər/) – Someone who is shy, introverted, or prefers to stay out of the spotlight at social events.
Example: "I'm more of a wallflower; I don't like being the center of attention."

Wasted (/ˈweɪstɪd/) – A term for being extremely drunk or intoxicated.
Example: "He was totally wasted after the party last night."

Wavy (/ˈweɪvi/) – Used to describe someone or something that's cool, stylish, or impressive.
Example: "Those new sneakers are wavy!"

Wig (/wɪg/) – Used to express amazement, excitement, or surprise, often implying that something was so impressive or shocking that it figuratively blew your hair off.
Example: "Did you see her performance? Wig!"

Whip (/wɪp/) – In slang, "whip" refers to a car, especially a luxury or sporty one. The term is believed to come from the old-fashioned use of a whip to control horse-drawn carriages, later being associated with the act of driving a car.
Example: "Check out his new whip—it's a sports car!"

Wildin' (/ˈwaɪldɪn/) – Acting out of control, unusually excited, or behaving recklessly.
Example: "You're wildin' if you think I'm going to that party."

Winter Arc (/ˈwɪntər ɑːrk/) – The "Winter Arc" is a viral trend popular among Gen Z, referring to the last 90 days of the year, where people focus on self-improvement, wellness, and personal growth. The Winter Arc often involves setting goals, working on mental health, and reflecting on the year before starting fresh.

Example: "I'm starting my Winter Arc now—focusing on meditation and hitting the gym before the new year."

Wojacks (/ˈwoʊdʒæks/) – A term used to refer to a popular internet meme that often depicts a sad or melancholic character. The meme is commonly used to express feelings of sadness, loneliness, or frustration, often in a relatable or humorous way.

Example: "After failing my exam again, I felt like a total Wojack—just scrolling through memes to forget about it."

Workation (/wɜːrˈkeɪʃən/) – A vacation taken with the intention of still working remotely while relaxing.

Example: "I'm going to the beach for a workation next week. Can't wait to be productive with a view."

Wifey (/ˈwaɪfi/) – A term of endearment for a girlfriend or partner who has the qualities of "wife material."

Example: "She's got that wifey vibe."

Whip Out (/wɪp aʊt/) – To bring out or use something quickly.

Example: "He whipped out his phone to take a video."

Where are the Avocados? (/wɛr ɑːr ðə ævəˌkɑːdəʊz/) – A playful or exaggerated phrase on social media to comment on a situation where something important is missing or out of stock.

Example: "We've been talking about change for months, but when it comes time to act—where are the avocados?"

Wizard (/ˈwɪzəd/) – Used to describe someone who is exceptionally skilled at something, often associated with video games or technology.

Example: "He's a total wizard at coding."

Xan (/zæn/) – Slang for Xanax, often used in the context of memes or rap lyrics, sometimes to refer to feeling relaxed or calm.
Example: "He was so chill, it was like he was on Xan."

X'ed (/ɛksd/) – A variant of *Punk'd*, but a PG-13 version of the word, coined by Jamie Kennedy. Refers to being pranked or tricked in a hidden-camera show format.
Example: "You see that sign over there? You've been X'ed. You're on my hidden-camera show, called The Jamie Kennedy Experiment. (Oh, shit!)"

X-Games Mode (/ɛks geɪmz moʊd/) – A phrase used to describe someone doing something extreme, intense, or impressive, often humorously exaggerating everyday achievements.
Example: "He finished that homework in five minutes; he was on X-Games mode."

XP (/ɛks pi/) – Short for "experience points," a term borrowed from gaming to mean gaining experience or life skills.
Example: "Moving out gave me so much XP in adulting."

XOXO (/ˌɛks oʊ ɛks oʊ/) – Used to convey affection, usually meaning "hugs and kisses." Although older, it's sometimes used by Gen Z in an ironic or playful way.
Example: "Thanks for the tea, XOXO!"

X-Y-Z-E (/ɛks waɪ zi:/) – Slang used to describe the feelings between two people that are more than "like" but not quite "love." It represents an ambiguous, in-between emotional connection where the exact nature of the relationship is uncertain.

Example: "I don't know what it is. Maybe it's love, maybe not. Whatever the case, I X-Y-Z-E you."

Yapping (/ˈjæpɪŋ/) – When someone talks excessively or in an annoying manner.
Example: "He's been yapping about his weekend plans for an hour now."

Yikes (/jaɪks/) – Used to express discomfort, embarrassment, or shock about something awkward or cringey.
Example: "He tried to dance and slipped—yikes!"

Yeet (/jiːt/) – An exclamation of excitement, energy, or approval. Also used as a verb meaning to throw something with force or enthusiasm.
Example: "He yeeted the ball across the field!"

You Do You (/juː duː juː/) – An expression of encouragement, telling someone to do what feels right for them without worrying about others.
Example: "If you don't want to go out, that's fine. You do you."

Youniverse (/ˈjuːnɪvɜːrs/) – A term used to describe the idea that someone sees the world revolving around themselves, often in a narcissistic or self-centered way.
Example: "She really thinks the whole world revolves around her, like she's the queen of her own youniverse."

Why you always yapping during the lectures?
Chill twin! I am trying to keep it entertaining

Z

Zaddy (/ˈzædi/) – An attractive, stylish man, often older, who exudes confidence and appeal.
Example: "Did you see him in that suit? Total zaddy vibes."

Zesty (/ˈzɛsti/) – Refers to something exciting, fresh, or full of energy.
Example: "His personality is so sesty; he really lights up the room."

Zen (/zɛn/) – Being calm, peaceful, and mindful.
Example: "I'm staying totally sen through all this chaos."

Zip It (/zɪp ɪt/) – A playful or blunt way to tell someone to be quiet or stop talking.
Example: "You're spoiling the ending – zip it!"

Zone Out (/zoʊn aʊt/) – To lose focus or daydream.
Example: "I totally zoned out during the lecture."

Zombied (/ˈzɒmbiːd/) – When someone ghosts you and then reappears out of nowhere, like a "ghost" coming back to life.
Example: "He stopped texting me for weeks, and then zombied me out of nowhere."

Zonked (/zɒŋkt/) – Extremely tired or exhausted.
Example: "After that hike, I'm completely zonked."

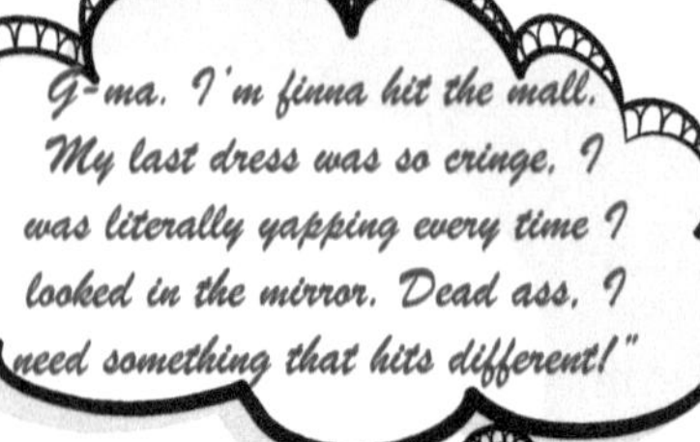
G-ma, I'm finna hit the mall. My last dress was so cringe, I was literally yapping every time I looked in the mirror. Dead ass, I need something that hits different!"

Hey, Zara! Where are you going?

Glossary to Gen Z/Alpha Acronyms

GEN Z/ALPHA ACRONYMS

AESTH: Aesthetic

Explanation: Used to describe style, vibe, or visual appeal.

Example: "Her room has such a cozy aesth."

AFK: Away from Keyboard

Explanation: Indicates that someone is temporarily not available online.

Example: "I'll be AFK for a bit, but I'll reply soon."

AFAIK: As Far as I Know

Explanation: Used to share knowledge while leaving room for uncertainty.

Example: "AFAIK, the event starts at 6."

AKA: Also Known As

Explanation: Used to introduce an alternative name or identity.

Example: "Michael Jordan, AKA MJ, is a basketball legend."

AMA: Ask Me Anything

Explanation: An invitation for open questions, often seen on social media or forums.

Example: "Just finished my trip; AMA!"

ASAP: As Soon As Possible
Explanation: Used to request something urgently.
Example: "Can you send me the files ASAP?"

ATM: At the Moment
Explanation: Indicates something happening right now or someone's current status.
Example: "I'm busy ATM; let's talk later."

ATMOS: Atmosphere
Explanation: Refers to the vibe or mood of a place or setting.
Example: "This café has such a cozy ATMOS."

AYKM: Are You Kidding Me?
Explanation: Used to express disbelief or shock.
Example: "AYKM? They really cancelled the show!"

ASL: Age, Sex, Location
Explanation: Originally used in online chats to ask someone for their age, sex, and location.
Example: "Hey, ASL?"

B

B2B: Business to Business
Explanation: Refers to transactions or relationships between two businesses.
Example: "Our company specializes in B2B software solutions."

B2C: Business to Consumer
Explanation: Refers to direct transactions between a business and individual consumer.
Example: "Amazon is a major player in the B2C market."

BAE: Before Anyone Else
Explanation: A term of endearment for a significant other.
Example: "Spending the day with my bae."

BFF: Best Friends Forever
Explanation: Used to describe a very close friend.
Example: "She's my BFF since grade school."

BRB: Be Right Back
Explanation: A quick way to indicate a short absence.
Example: "Hold on, BRB."

BSAAW: Big Smile and a Wink
Explanation: Used to convey a friendly and playful tone.
Example: "Great work on the project, BSAAW!"

BTW: By the Way
Explanation: Used to introduce additional or supplementary information.
Example: "BTW, I finished the project you asked for."

BOP: Good Song
Explanation: Used to describe a catchy or great song.
Example: "This new track is such a bop!"

BWL: Bursting With Laughter
Explanation: Used to describe laughing uncontrollably.
Example: "That joke was hilarious, I'm BWL."

BRUH: A Term of Exasperation or Disbelief
Explanation: An expression of surprise or frustration, commonly used in conversations.
Example: "Bruh, did you really just do that?"

BTAIM: Be That As It May
Explanation: Used to acknowledge something but move on or present a contrasting viewpoint.
Example: "BTAIM, we still need to finish this project by tomorrow."

C

CBA: Can't Be Bothered
Explanation: Used to express a lack of interest or willingness to do something.
Example: "I CBA to go out tonight."

CMB: Call Me Back
Explanation: A request to return a phone call.
Example: "Leave a message, and I'll CMB later."

CMGR: Community Manager
Explanation: Refers to a person responsible for managing and engaging with an online community.
Example: "Our CMGR organizes events to keep the group active."

CMS: Content Management System
Explanation: A software platform for managing digital content, often for websites.
Example: "We use a CMS to update our blog posts."

COB: Close of Business
Explanation: Refers to the end of the business day.
Example: "Please send the report by COB today."

CSL: Can't Stop Laughing
Explanation: Indicates something extremely funny.
Example: "That joke was hilarious—CSL!"

CTA: Call to Action
Explanation: A prompt encouraging the audience to take a specific action, such as clicking a link or making a purchase.
Example: "The ad's CTA was effective in boosting sales."

CMV: Change My View

Explanation: Used to challenge someone to present an argument that could alter the current perspective or opinion.

Example: "CMV, social media has done more harm than good to society."

CTN: Can't Talk Now

Explanation: Indicates that the person is unable to talk at the moment.

Example: "Sorry, CTN. I'll call you back in 10 minutes."

CU: See You

Explanation: A casual way to say goodbye.

Example: "I've got to go. CU!"

CUA: See You Around

Explanation: Another informal way to say goodbye, often used when you plan to see someone again.

Example: "It was fun hanging out. CUA!"

CUL: See You Later

Explanation: A casual farewell, implying that you'll see the person at a later time.

Example: "I'm heading out now, CUL!"

CYA: See Ya

Explanation: A shortened version of "see you," commonly used in text or online communication.

Example: "I'm off to bed, CYA!"

DAE: Does Anyone Else
Explanation: A way to start a conversation or find others who share the same experience.
Example: "DAE get nervous speaking in meetings?"

DM: Direct Message
Explanation: A private message sent on social media platforms.
Example: "If you have questions, feel free to DM me."

DNI: Do Not Interact
Explanation: A request to avoid engagement, often seen on social media profiles.
Example: "If you don't support inclusivity, DNI with my posts."

DIY: Do It Yourself
Explanation: Refers to creating or fixing things on your own, often seen in crafting and home improvement.
Example: "I love watching DIY videos for room decor ideas."

DND: Do Not Disturb
Explanation: Indicates that someone does not want to be interrupted or contacted.
Example: "Setting my phone to DND so I can focus on studying."

DTF: Down to (Have Fun)
Explanation: A slang term expressing openness to hanging out or other activities.
Example: "Are you DTF for some weekend plans?"

DTR: Define the Relationship

Explanation: Used to talk about clarifying relationship status with a partner.

Example: "We had the DTR conversation, and now we're officially dating."

DW: Don't Worry

Explanation: Used to reassure someone that everything is okay.

Example: "DW about the deadline; I've got it covered."

DWU: Don't Wait Up

Explanation: Used to let someone know they don't need to stay awake or wait for you.

Example: "I'll be home late tonight, DWU."

DFTBA: Don't Forget To Be Awesome

Explanation: A positive reminder to stay awesome and confident.

Example: "Heading into the new week, DFTBA!"

EOD: End of Discussion
Explanation: Used to indicate that a topic is closed for further debate.
Example: "I've made up my mind on this. EOD."

ELI5: Explain Like I'm 5
Explanation: A request to simplify an explanation, as if speaking to a young child.
Example: "I don't understand this at all—can you ELI5?"

ESP: Extrasensory Perception
Explanation: Used humorously to refer to knowing something without being told, like a "sixth sense."
Example: "I knew you'd say that! Must be ESP."

ETA: Edited To Add
Explanation: Used in online posts to add extra information after the original post.
Example: "ETA: Forgot to mention, it's potluck style."

ETA: Estimated Time of Arrival
Explanation: Used to ask or share when someone expects to arrive.
Example: "What's your ETA? The movie starts in 10 minutes."

EWF: Earth, Wind, and Fire
Explanation: Refers to the popular music group, but also shorthand for a vibe or throwback mood.
Example: "Playing some EWF tonight for good vibes."

EZ: Easy
Explanation: Slang for something simple or quick to do.
Example: "That test was EZ; I finished in 10 minutes."

EYEY: Yeah Yeah (pronounced as letters "E-Y-E-Y")
Explanation: An expression to show agreement or acknowledgement in a casual, playful way.
Example: "Are you coming to the party? EYEY!"

FAQ: Frequently Asked Questions
Explanation: A list of common questions and answers about a topic, sometimes used jokingly.
Example: "Check my FAQ before you ask why I'm single!"

FB: Follow Back
Explanation: A request for someone to follow you back on social media.
Example: "Just followed you! FB?"

FOMO: Fear of Missing Out
Explanation: The feeling of anxiety over missing exciting events or social activities.
Example: "Everyone's going on that trip, and my FOMO is real!"

FTW: For The Win
Explanation: Used to indicate something excellent or that leads to success.
Example: "Pizza party FTW!"

FR: For Real
Explanation: Used to express sincerity or emphasis.
Example: "That movie was scary, FR!"

FTL: For The Loss
Explanation: Used to describe something disappointing or unfavorable.
Example: "Rain on a beach day? FTL."

FWIW: For What It's Worth
Explanation: Used to add a personal opinion, often to soften it.
Example: "FWIW, I think you should go for it!"

FYI: For Your Information
Explanation: Used to share relevant information or updates.
Example: "FYI, the deadline was extended to Monday."

F2F: Face to Face
Explanation: Used when meeting someone in person instead of online or
Example:"Let's catch up F2F soon!"

FWB: Friends with Benefits
Explanation: A friendship that includes romantic or physical aspects without a committed relationship.
Example:"They're just FWB, no strings attached."

FTFY: Fixed That For You
Explanation: Used humorously to correct or improve a previous statement.
Example:"You meant 'best band ever,' FTFY."

G

GOAT: Greatest of All Time
Explanation: Used to refer to someone or something that is the best in its field.
Example:"LeBron is the GOAT of basketball!"

GRWM: Get Ready With Me
Explanation: A popular video format, often used on social media, where someone shows their routine.
Example:"Posting a GRWM for my first day at college."

GTG: Got To Go
Explanation: Used to say goodbye or leave a conversation quickly.
Example:"Sorry, GTG, my phone's about to die."

G2G: Good To Go
Explanation: Indicates that someone is ready to proceed or start.
Example:"I've packed everything; I'm G2G!"

GMTA: Great Minds Think Alike
Explanation: Used when two people have the same thought or idea.
Example:"You ordered pizza too? GMTA!"

GLHF: Good Luck, Have Fun
Explanation: Often used before online games or competitions to wish others well.
Example: "Joining the game now, GLHF!"

GF: Good Friend (or also Girlfriend)
Explanation: Can refer to a close friend or a romantic partner.
Example:"Just hanging out with my GF this weekend."

GN: Good Night
Explanation: A way to say goodbye at night, often in messages.
Example:"I'm exhausted. GN, everyone!"

GNSD: Good Night Sweet Dreams
Explanation: A phrase used to wish someone a peaceful and pleasant sleep.
Example:"Heading to bed, GNSD! Sleep well!"

GOI: Get Over It
Explanation: Used to tell someone to stop dwelling on something.
Example:"I know you're upset, but it's time to GOI."

GYAT: Get Your Act Together
Explanation: A phrase used to encourage someone to focus or be responsible.
Example:"Your deadline's tomorrow; GYAT!"

GTR: Getting Ready
Explanation: Used to inform someone that you're getting prepared for something.
Example:"I'll be there soon, just GTR."

GTFO: Get The Freak Out
Explanation: A stronger, sometimes humorous way to tell someone to leave or express disbelief.
Example:"She's moving to New York? GTFO!"

HMB: Hit Me Back
Explanation: A request to respond or get in touch.
Example: "Hey, HMB when you're free!"

HMU: Hit Me Up
Explanation: An invitation to contact or reach out to someone.
Example: "HMU if you want to hang out later."

HRU: How Are You
Explanation: A casual way of asking someone how they're doing.
Example: "Hey, HRU? It's been a while!"

HIFW: How I Feel When
Explanation: Used to express emotions or reactions to a specific situation.
Example: "HIFW I finish a good book and don't know what to read next."

HOM: Hype Over Me
Explanation: Used to indicate being overwhelmed by attention or excitement.
Example: "I'm not ready for all the HOM at the party tonight!"

HODL: Hold on for Dear Life
Explanation: Used in reference to keeping a strong position, often in the context of investments or cryptocurrency.

Example: "I'm just going to HODL my stocks, even with the market drop."

HAGS: Have A Great Summer
Explanation: A casual goodbye message during the summer.
Example: "Finals are over, HAGS, everyone!"

HYD: Have You Done?
Explanation: A quick way to ask if someone has completed a task or goal.
Example: "HYD with your homework yet?"

HNB: Hype Not Needed
Explanation: Used to say there's no need to overhype something.
Example: "That movie wasn't as good as they said. HNB."

HOA: Hold On A Second
Explanation: A phrase used to ask for a pause or moment of patience.
Example: "HOA, let me finish this real quick."

ICYMI: In Case You Missed It
Explanation: Used to bring attention to something that someone may have overlooked.
Example: "ICYMI, the meeting was moved to Thursday."

IDK: I Don't Know
Explanation: Expresses lack of knowledge about a topic.
Example: "IDK where he went."

IDC: I Don't Care
Explanation: Shows indifference or lack of concern.
Example: "IDC about what others think."

IFYP: I Feel Your Pain
Explanation: Conveys empathy or understanding of someone's struggle.
Example: "Stuck in traffic? IFYP."

IG: Instagram
Explanation: Refers to the social media platform Instagram.
Example: "I posted the pictures on IG."

IKR: I Know, Right?
Explanation: Used to express agreement with something that was said.
Example: "That movie was amazing! IKR?"

ILY: I Love You
Explanation: A term of affection or love.
Example: "Goodnight, ILY!"

IM: Instant Message
Explanation: A real-time message sent via an online chat system.
Example: "Just send me an IM if you're online."

IMO: In My Opinion
Explanation: Used to introduce a personal perspective or belief.
Example: "IMO, the first season was the best."

IMHO: In My Humble Opinion
Explanation: Used to share a personal opinion, often modestly.
Example: "IMHO, they should have called first."

IRL: In Real Life
Explanation: Refers to experiences outside of the online or virtual world.
Example: "We finally met IRL last week."

ISTG: I Swear To God
Explanation: Used to emphasise the seriousness or sincerity of a statement.
Example: "ISTG, that was the funniest thing I've ever seen!"

IYKYK: If You Know, You Know
Explanation: Used when something is understood only by a specific group of people who share the same knowledge or experience.
Example: "The party was lit last night, but IYKYK, if you weren't there, you wouldn't understand."

J

JOMO: Joy of Missing Out
Explanation: The pleasure or satisfaction derived from avoiding social events or distractions.
Example: "I'm staying home tonight, enjoying my JOMO."

JIT: Just In Time
Explanation: Something arriving or happening exactly when needed or expected.
Example: "I got to the meeting JIT, just before it started."

JK: Just Kidding
Explanation: Used to indicate that something said was meant as a joke or not seriously intended.
Example: "You're so bad at this game! JK, you're actually doing great!"

K: Okay
Explanation: A casual way of saying "okay" to acknowledge something.
Example: "I'll meet you at 7, K?"

KMS: Kill Myself (figuratively)
Explanation: Used to express extreme frustration, embarrassment, or exhaustion. Note: This acronym should be used with care as it can be sensitive or triggering.
Example: "I failed my test again, KMS."

KK: Okay, Okay
Explanation: A more enthusiastic or quick way of saying "okay."
Example: "You got it, KK."

KFY: Kiss For You
Explanation: A playful expression of affection or admiration.
Example: "Good luck on your exam, KFY!"

KYS: Kill Yourself (figuratively)
Explanation: A darkly humorous expression of frustration or annoyance. Like "KMS," it is often used hyperbolically but should be used with caution.
Example: "This homework is so hard, KYS."

KTL: Kill The Lights
Explanation: A phrase used when you're enjoying the vibe or mood of a party or event.
Example: "The party's lit, KTL!"

KNE: Knocked 'Em Out

Explanation: Used when someone achieves something impressively or effortlessly.

Example: "I just aced that test, KNE!"

KSC: Keep Some Change

Explanation: Used when someone gives extra change or money for a good tip or gesture.

Example: "Here's the bill, KSC!"

KTHNX: OK, Thanks

Explanation: A shorthand way to express gratitude or acknowledgment, often used in a casual or quick response.

Example: "KTHNX for helping me with the report."

LBR: Let's Be Real
Explanation: Used to signal honesty or to say something straightforward.
Example: "LBR, that outfit isn't working for you."

LMK: Let Me Know
Explanation: Used to request someone to inform you or give you an update.
Example: "LMK if you're free to hang out later."

LMSO: Laughing My Socks Off
Explanation: A playful variation of "LMAO" to show extreme amusement.
Example: "That cat video made me LMSO!"

LOL: Laugh Out Loud
Explanation: Used to show something is funny or amusing.
Example: "That joke was so good, LOL!"

LIT: Exciting or Excellent
Explanation: Used to describe something that is very exciting, impressive, or fun.
Example: "That party was so LIT last night."

L8R: Later
Explanation: Used to say goodbye or express that you'll talk to someone later.
Example: "Got to go, talk to you L8R."

LMS: Like My Status

Explanation: A request for others to like your social media status.

Example: "LMS if you agree with me."

LDR: *Long Distance Relationship*

Explanation: A relationship where the partners are geographically separated.

Example: "We're managing the LDR, but it's tough."

LULZ: *Laughs*

Explanation: A variant of "LOL," often used to refer to something that is amusing.

Example: "That prank was hilarious, LULZ."

MCM: Man Crush Monday
Explanation: A hashtag or term used on social media to express admiration or affection for a male celebrity, friend, or significant other, typically posted on Mondays.
Example: "Here's my MCM this week – Chris Hemsworth!"

MIA: Missing in Action
Explanation: Used to describe someone who is absent or hard to reach, often without explanation.
Example: "Where's Sarah? She's been MIA all day."

MFW: My Face When
Explanation: Used to describe a facial expression or reaction in response to something.
Example: "MFW I saw my exam results."

MTFBWY: May The Force Be With You
Explanation: A phrase used to wish someone good luck or success, especially in a challenging situation, often associated with the "Star Wars" franchise.
Example: "Good luck on your presentation today, MTFBWY!"

MVP: Most Valuable Player
Explanation: Often used in gaming or sports to refer to the person who performed the best or contributed the most.
Example: "You're the MVP of our team, thanks for carrying us."

MYOB: Mind Your Own Business
Explanation: Used to tell someone to stop interfering or asking questions about something personal.
Example: "Why are you asking so many questions? MYOB."

M.I.R.L: Meet in Real Life

Explanation: Refers to meeting someone in person after interacting online.

Example:"We've been chatting online for months, I think it's time for a M.I.R.L."

MKAY: Mmm, okay

Explanation: A casual or slightly reluctant acknowledgment of understanding or agreement.

Example:"Mkay, I guess I'll go along with it."

MUA: Make-Up Artist

Explanation: Refers to a professional who applies makeup to individuals, typically for events or photoshoots.

Example:"I need to book an MUA for the wedding!"

NVM: Never Mind
Explanation: Indicates that something previously mentioned or asked about is no longer relevant.
Example: "NVM, I found the keys."

NSFW: Not Safe for Work
Explanation: Used to indicate that content may be inappropriate for a professional setting or workplace.
Example: "Don't open that link at work, it's NSFW."

NBD: No Big Deal
Explanation: Used to downplay something, indicating it's not important or isn't a problem.
Example: "Don't worry about it, it's NBD."

NGL: Not Gonna Lie
Explanation: Used to preface a statement that is honest or blunt.
Example: "NGL, I don't really like that movie."

NOOB: Newbie
Explanation: Refers to someone who is inexperienced or new to something.
Example: "Stop acting like a noob, just press the button."

NVM: Never Mind
Explanation: Indicates that something previously mentioned or asked about is no longer relevant.
Example: "NVM, I found the keys."

NM: Not Much
Explanation: Used to indicate that nothing significant is going on or to answer a question about what someone is doing.
Example: "What's up?" "NM, just chilling."

NSFL: Not Safe For Life
Explanation: Used to indicate content that is extremely disturbing or graphic.
Example: "That video was NSFL, I had to turn it off."

NOM: Nom Nom
Explanation: Used to express enjoyment of food, often written as *nom nom* to imitate the sound of eating.
Example: "This pizza is so good, *nom nom!*"

NUT: Crazy or Wild
Explanation: Used to describe something that is extreme or over the top.
Example: "That party was NUT last night."

OMG: Oh My God
Explanation: Used to express surprise, shock, or excitement.
Example: "OMG, I can't believe you won!"

OMW: On My Way
Explanation: Used to inform someone that you are en route.
Example: "I'm OMW to the party!"

Oomf: One of My Followers
Explanation: Abbreviation for "One of My Followers," typically used on social media to refer to a follower or someone who engages with your content.
Example: "Oomf just shared my post, that's so sweet!"

OOO: Out of Office
Explanation: Used when someone is not at work or unavailable.
Example: "I'm OOO today, back on Monday."

OAN: On Another Note
Explanation: Used to shift the conversation to a new topic.
Example: "OAN, have you heard about the new movie?"

OP: Original Poster
Explanation: Refers to the person who started a post or thread online.
Example: "The OP didn't mention the details."

OOTD: Outfit of The Day
Explanation: Used to share or describe the outfit someone is wearing for the day, often used on social media.
Example: "Here's my OOTD, feeling stylish today!"

ORLY: Oh Really?!

Explanation: Used to express surprise, disbelief, or interest in what someone has just said.

Example:"You're going to Paris next week? ORLY?"

P2P: Peer to Peer
Explanation: Refers to direct interaction between individuals without intermediaries.
Example:"This is a P2P lending platform."

PFP: Profile Picture
Explanation: Refers to the image that represents someone's online identity.
Example:"I just changed my PFP on Facebook."

PG: Parental Guidance
Explanation: to imply that something is "safe" or "acceptable" in a non-controversial way.
Example: "This movie is rated PG, so it's safe for the whole family, but there are a couple of scary scenes that might be a little intense for younger kids."

PLS: Please
Explanation: A shorthand used for requesting something politely.
Example: "PLS send me the link."

POTD: Photo of the Day
Explanation: A popular post shared as the highlight of the day.
Example: "Check out my POTD on Instagram!"

PPL: People
Explanation: A shorthand way to refer to a group of individuals.
Example: "These PPL are amazing."

PR: Public Relations
Explanation: The practice of managing information between an organization and the public.
Example: "She works in PR and handles all the media queries."

PMA: Positive Mental Attitude
Explanation: Refers to staying optimistic and focused.
Example: "Always keep a PMA and things will improve."

POV: Point of View
Explanation: Refers to a perspective or opinion.
Example: "From my POV, it's a great idea."

PTAT: People Talk About That
Explanation: Used to describe something that is trending or generating a lot of conversation.
Example: "Did you hear the news about the concert? It's PTAT right now."

PP: Profile Picture
Explanation: Refers to the image or photo that represents a person on social media or messaging platforms.
Example: "I just changed my PP to a new selfie!"

QA: Question and Answer
Explanation: Refers to a session or format where questions are asked and answered.
Example: "Let's do a QA after the presentation!"

QAF: Question and Answer Format
Explanation: Refers to a style or format for asking and answering questions.
Example: "Let's do this in QAF for clarity."

Q&D: Quick and Dirty
Explanation: Refers to a style of problem-solving or work that is done quickly and without attention to detail, often to save time or avoid extensive planning. It can also be used as a form of plausible deniability.
Example: "So my boss told me to just do it Q&D."

QIK: Quick
Explanation: Shortened form of the word "quick."
Example: "I need a QIK reply!"

QOTD: Quote Of The Day
Explanation: A daily quote shared for inspiration or reflection.
Example: "QOTD: 'Believe in yourself!'"

QR: Quick Response
Explanation: Often used in reference to QR codes or to describe a fast reply or action.
Example: "Scan the QR code to learn more!"

QS: Quick Shout
Explanation: Used to quickly call out or recognise something or someone.
Example: "QS to my bestie for helping me out!"

QST: Question
Explanation: A shorthand used for asking a question.
Example: "Got a QST for you – what's your favourite movie?"

QT: Cutie
Explanation: A term of endearment for someone who is cute or attractive.
Example: "Hey QT, looking great today!"

QTI: Quoted Text Information
Explanation: Used when referencing or sharing text that's been quoted.
Example: "Here's the QTI from the article I was talking about."

QWERTY: Keyboard
Explanation: Referring to the standard layout of keys on a keyboard, often used when typing online.
Example: "I accidentally hit the wrong key on the QWERTY!"

RBF: Resting Bitch Face
Explanation: A facial expression that unintentionally appears angry or annoyed, even when the person is not.
Example: "She didn't mean to look upset, it's just her RBF."

R D & S: Really Depressed and Suicidal
Explanation: A term used to describe a state of intense sadness and hopelessness, often associated with thoughts of self-harm or suicide.
Example: "Today wasn't a great day, feel R D & S."

RIP: Rest in Peace
Explanation: A phrase used to show respect for someone who has passed away.
Example: "RIP to my favourite celebrity."

ROFL: Rolling On the Floor Laughing
Explanation: Used to express that something is extremely funny.
Example: "That meme was so funny, I'm ROFL."

ROFLMAO: Rolling On the Floor Laughing My Ass Off
Explanation: A more intense version of "ROFL," used to express extreme amusement.
Example: "That video had me ROFLMAO!"

RN: Right Now
Explanation: Used to indicate something is happening in the present moment.
Example: "I'm too busy RN, can we talk later?"

RSVP: Répondez s'il vous plaît (French for "Please respond")
Explanation: Used to request a response to an invitation.
Example: "Don't forget to RSVP to the wedding invite."

RT: Retweet
Explanation: To share someone else's tweet on Twitter.
Example: "I RT'd your post, it's great!"

S2S: Soul to Soul

Explanation: Used to describe a deep, meaningful connection between two people.

Example: "We had an amazing conversation, just S2S."

S/O: Shout Out

Explanation: A public expression of gratitude or recognition.

Example: "Big S/O to everyone who helped with the project!"

SMH: Shaking My Head

Explanation: Used to show disbelief, disappointment, or frustration at something.

Example: "She actually did that? SMH."

SME / SM: Same

Explanation: Used as shorthand to indicate something is the same as previously mentioned.

Example: "That's SME, I feel the same way."

S'MORE: Some More

Explanation: Refers to wanting or asking for more of something, often used in informal contexts.

Example: "Can I have s'more cookies?"

SRS: Serious

Explanation: Used to emphasise that something is not a joke or is of importance.

Example: "I'm SRS, don't mess with me right now."

SRSLY: Seriously
Explanation: Used to express disbelief or emphasise something important.
Example: "Srsly, how did you not know that?"

SSDD: Same Stuff, Different Day
Explanation: Used to express that nothing has changed and things are repetitive or dull.
Example: "Work was SSDD today, just the usual tasks."

SUX: Sucks or "It sucks"
Explanation: Used to express dissatisfaction or disappointment.
Example: "That movie was so boring, it sux."

SUS: Suspicious
Explanation: Used to describe something or someone that seems shady or untrustworthy.
Example: "He's been acting all sus lately, I don't know if I trust him."

SRY: Sorry
Explanation: An abbreviation for apologizing.
Example: "Sry I'm late, I missed the bus."

TBA: To Be Announced
Explanation: Used when the details of something are not yet revealed.
Example: "The date for the event is TBA."

TBF: To Be Fair
Explanation: Used to introduce a fair or balanced point.
Example: "TBF, he did try his best."

TBT: Throwback Thursday
Explanation: A social media trend where people post old photos or memories on Thursdays.
Example: "Here's my TBT from last summer!"

TBH: To Be Honest
Explanation: Used to preface a candid or frank opinion.
Example: "TBH, I don't like that movie."

TFC: The FOMO Club
Explanation: A humorous reference to the feeling of missing out on something.
Example: "I didn't get invited to the party, I guess I'm in the TFC."

TGIF: Thank God It's Friday
Explanation: Used to express relief or excitement for the weekend.
Example: "It's been a long week, but TGIF!"

TIME: Tears in My Eyes
Explanation: Used to express overwhelming emotions, often due to laughter or sadness.
Example: "That movie was so funny, I literally had TIME!"

TMI: Too Much Information
Explanation: Used when someone shares more details than necessary or wanted.
Example: "That's TMI, I didn't need to know that!"

TMIY: Tell Me If You
Explanation: A shorthand used to ask someone to inform you if they know something or can do something.
Example: "TMIY if you hear anything about the job opening."

TNTL: Trying Not to Laugh
Explanation: Used when something is so funny that you are trying hard not to laugh.
Example: "That joke was so good, I'm TNTL right now!"

TL; DR: Too Long; Didn't Read
Explanation: Used to summarise or indicate that something is too lengthy to read in full.
Example: "TL; DR – We're going to the beach this weekend."

TTFN: Ta-ta for now
Explanation: A casual way to say goodbye, implying you'll talk again later.
Example: "I have to go, TTFN!"

TTYL: Talk to You Later
Explanation: Used to say goodbye or indicate that the conversation will end for now.
Example: "I've got to go now, TTYL!"

TWF: That Feeling When
Explanation: Used to describe a specific emotion or reaction triggered by a situation, often shared in relatable experiences.
Example: "TWF you finally finish a big project and can relax!"

TIA: Thanks in Advance
Explanation: Used to show appreciation before receiving help or a favour.
Example: "TIA for sending me the notes!"

UO: Unpopular Opinion
Explanation: Used to share a personal opinion that may differ from mainstream beliefs.
Example: "UO, but I think coffee is overrated."

UWU: Expressing Cuteness or Affection
Explanation: Often used in text or meme culture to convey feelings of adorableness.
Example: "That puppy is so adorable, UWU!"

USG: You're So Good
Explanation: A compliment, typically in gaming or creative contexts.
Example: "USG at making TikToks!"

UHU: Unintentionally Hilarious Update
Explanation: Describes an unexpected or accidental funny post or message.
Example: "That typo in your message was a total UHU!"

UMM: Unofficial Meme Moment
Explanation: Used when something unintentionally becomes meme-worthy.
Example: "That awkward photo is such a UMM!"

UD: Urban Dictionary
Explanation: Refers to the online slang and phrase dictionary.
Example: "I had to check UD to understand what 'no cap' means."

UR: Your or You Are

Explanation: A shorthand version of "your" or "you are," commonly used in texting.

Example: "UR amazing at this!"

UNO: You're Not Okay

Explanation: Used playfully or sarcastically to point out when someone's being extra.

Example: "Did you just eat pizza with ketchup? UNO!"

V: Very
Explanation: A shorthand for "very," often used in casual messages.
Example: "That movie was V intense!"

VSCO: Aesthetic Style or Culture
Explanation: Refers to the aesthetic linked to the photo editing app VSCO, often associated with trendy "VSCO girls."
Example: "Her outfit is giving total VSCO vibes."

VFL: Vibes For Life
Explanation: A phrase used to describe someone's strong positive energy or vibe.
Example: "That sunset pic is VFL-worthy!"

VBD: Very Big Deal
Explanation: A way of emphasizing something important or significant.
Example: "Landing that internship is a VBD!"

VIBES: Very Important Besties Encouraging Support
Explanation: Playfully used to describe a close-knit, positive friend group.
Example: "Our group chat is full of good VIBES!"

W8: Wait
Explanation: A shorthand version of the word "wait," often used in texting.
Example: "W8 for me, I'm almost there!"

WB: Welcome Back
Explanation: Used to greet someone who has returned.
Example: "Hey, WB! Long time no see."

WCW: Woman Crush Wednesday
Explanation: A hashtag used on social media to express admiration or affection for a female celebrity, friend, or significant other, typically posted on Wednesdays.
Example: "My WCW this week is Zendaya!"

WBU: What About You?
Explanation: A casual way to ask someone about their opinion or situation after sharing yours.
Example: "I'm doing great, WBU?"

W/E: Whatever
Explanation: A casual dismissal of something; can indicate indifference.
Example: "W/E, I'm not bothered."

WDYMBT: What Do You Mean By That?
Explanation: A phrase used to ask for clarification when something said is unclear or confusing.
Example: "You're going to the party alone? WDYMBT?"

WFM: Working From Home

Explanation: Refers to the practice of performing job tasks remotely from one's home instead of commuting to a traditional office.

Example: "I'll be WFM today, so just text me if you need anything."

WGYW: Wish You Were Here

Explanation: Used to express longing or missing someone or something.

Example: "The party's so much fun, WYWH!"

WTF: What The F***?

Explanation: Used to express confusion, anger, or surprise.

Example: "WTF is going on here?"

WTH: What The Heck?

Explanation: An expression of surprise, shock, or disbelief.

Example: "WTH just happened?"

WYM: What You Mean?

Explanation: Asking for clarification on something said.

Example: "I don't get what you're saying, WYM?"

WAG: Wives And Girlfriends

Explanation: Refers to the partners of athletes, typically used in sports media.

Example: "The WAGs were all sitting together at the game."

WRK: Work

Explanation: Refers to one's job, tasks, or professional activities.

Example: "I've got to get back to WRK now."

WTG: Way to Go

Explanation: A phrase used to express praise or congratulations.

Example: "You passed the exam? WTG!"

WYD / WUD: What You Doing?

Explanation: A casual way to ask someone what they are currently doing or how they are spending their time.

Example: "Hey, WYD?" or "WUD, wanna hang out later?"

WYWD / WUWD: What You Wanna Do?

Explanation: A casual way of asking someone what they would like to do or what their plans are.

Example: "It's Saturday, WYWD?" or "We have some free time, WUWD?"

WYSIWYG: What You See Is What You Get

Explanation: Refers to something that appears exactly as it is, especially in computing or design.

Example: "This editor is WYSIWYG, so you can see the final result as you work."

XOXO: Hugs and Kisses
Explanation: Used to express affection, good friendship, or love.
Example: "Goodnight, XOXO!"

X-Factor
Explanation: Refers to a noteworthy special talent or quality that makes someone stand out.
Example: "She's got the X-factor, no doubt!"

YAAAS: Yes
Explanation: A more enthusiastic and drawn-out form of "yes," used to express excitement or approval.
Example: "YAAAS, I love this song!"

YAS: Yes
Explanation: Used to express excitement or agreement.
Example: "YAS! That new movie was amazing!"

YDT: You Do The
Explanation: Often used in the context of challenges or memes, asking the other person to perform an action.
Example: "YDT for the challenge video!"

YEP: Yes
Explanation: Informal and quick way of saying yes.
Example: "Are we still meeting later? YEP!"

YFI: Your Friend Is
Explanation: Used in social contexts when sharing experiences involving friends.
Example: "YFI, she just started a new job."

YIKES
Explanation: Used to express shock or concern about something.
Example: "YIKES, that test was way harder than I expected!"

YNK: You Never Know

Explanation: Used to express uncertainty or to imply that anything is possible.

Example: "He might actually show up to the party, YNK!"

YOLO: You Only Live Once

Explanation: Used to encourage taking risks or living life to the fullest.

Example: "I'm going skydiving tomorrow, YOLO!"

YMMV: Your Mileage May Vary

Explanation: Used to indicate that different people may have different experiences or results.

Example: "The food was great, but YMMV depending on the chef."

YSK: You Should Know

Explanation: Used to preface information that the speaker believes is important or helpful.

Example: "YSK, the event starts at 7 pm, not 6."

YWW: You Were Warned

Explanation: Used when someone ignores advice or a warning and then faces the consequences.

Example: "I told you not to eat that much, YWW."

ZB: Zero Balance

Explanation: A financial term indicating that an account or transaction has no balance remaining.

Example: "Your account shows a ZB; please add funds to proceed."

ZBAG: Zillion Billionaire Awkward Grin

Explanation: A humorous term for someone who has an overwhelming amount of wealth but still behaves awkwardly.

Example: "He's the ZBAG of the company but can't talk to anyone without blushing."

ZK: Zero Knowledge

Explanation: A term in cryptography referring to a proof that a statement is true without revealing any information about the statement itself.

Example: "The blockchain system uses ZK to ensure privacy."

ZOMG: Oh My God (intensified)

Explanation: An exaggerated form of "OMG," used to express surprise or excitement.

Example: "ZOMG, I can't believe we won the lottery!"

ZQ: Zero Queue

Explanation: Refers to a situation where there is no waiting line or backlog, often used in customer service contexts.

Example: "Great, there's a ZQ at the customer support desk today!"

ZTL: Zombie Time Limit

Explanation: Refers to a deadline or time limit that seems unreasonably long or stretched out, often used humorously.

Example: "I've got until ZTL to finish this task."

Reference

Dillman, Theodora. *Teen Slang Dictionary*. CPYU, Nov. 2020, https://cpyu.org/wp-content/uploads/2020/11/Teen-Slang-Dictionary.pdf.

"Gen Z is Talking – Are You Listening?" *PwC*, 2023, https://www.pwc.de/de/handel-und-konsumguter/gen-z-is-talking-are-you-listening.pdf.

"Gen Z Slang." *Urban Dictionary*, 2024, www.urbandictionary.com.

"Gen Z Slang Words." *GeeksforGeeks*, https://geeksforgeeks.org/gen-z-slang-words/.

Generation Z Dictionary. District Deeds, May 2019, https://districtdeeds.blog/wp-content/uploads/2019/05/generation-z-dictionary.pdf.

Iberdrola. *Generation Alpha Will Lead a 100% Digital World*. Iberdrola, https://www.iberdrola.com/talent/alpha-generation.

International Institute of Professional Studies. "The Changing Face of Generation Z: Impact and Strategies." *IIP Series*, 2024, www.iipseries.org/assets/docupload/rsl20244A1B6A824E538F5.pdf.

Knye, L. Karbo. *How to Speak Gen Z*. Michigan State University, 2021, https://comms.msu.edu/-/media/assets/comms/docs/social-media/meetings-workshops/2021-02/202102-knye-lkarbo-how-to-speak-gen-z-2021.pdf.

"List of Generation Z Slang." *Wikipedia*, https://en.wikipedia.org/wiki/List_of_Generation_Z_slang.

McCrindle, Mark. "Generation Alpha: Understanding the Next Cohort of University Students." *European Journal of Contemporary Education*, vol. 10, no. 3, 2021, pp. 783-790, https://doi.org/10.13187/ejced.2021.3.783.

Generation Beta Defined." McCrindle, 2025, https://mccrindle.com.au/article/generation-beta-defined/. Accessed 9 Jan. 2025.

"Meet the Mini Millennials: Generation Alpha." *Poole Thought Leadership*, 1 Oct. 2021, poole.ncsu.edu/thought-leadership/generation-alpha.

"Words from the 1920s." *Oxford English Dictionary*, Oxford University Press, accessed 13 Nov. 2024, www.oed.com/discover/words-from-the-1920s.

"Words from the 1940s." *Oxford English Dictionary*, Oxford University Press, accessed 13 Nov. 2024, www.oed.com/discover/words-from-the-1940s.

"Words from the 1950s." *Oxford English Dictionary*, Oxford University Press, accessed 13 Nov. 2024, www.oed.com/discover/words-from-the-1950s.

"Z Slang." *Gen Alpha Slang*, https://genalphaslang.info/gen-z-slang/words/z.

Ymer Digital. "The Future of Work and Gen Z: Understanding Their Needs and Preferences." *Ymer Digital*, 2021, www.ymerdigital.com/uploads/YMER210152.pdf.

www.ingramcontent.com/pod-product-compliance
Lightning Source LLC
Chambersburg PA
CBHW021402150726
47989CB00005B/2359